CW00870773

EARNING IN RETIREMENT

Kenneth Lysons

BOOKS

© 1992 Kenneth Lysons
Published by Age Concern England
1268 London Road
London SW16 4ER

Editor   Caroline Hartnell
Design   Eugenie Dodd
Production   Marion Peat
Typesetting   Joyce O'Shaughnessy
Printed and bound in Great Britain by
Stephens & George Ltd, Merthyr Tydfil

A catalogue record for this book is available
from the British Library

ISBN 0–86242–103–9

Contents

Sponsor's foreword

Esso is delighted to be able to sponsor this book as part of the celebrations of Age Concern's Golden Jubilee.

Esso has always taken a close interest in all aspects of the welfare of its pensioners and has encouraged them to remain active in retirement. It gives us considerable pleasure, therefore, to sponsor a publication aimed at enabling people to go on earning in retirement.

Sir Archibald Forster
Chairman and Chief Executive
Esso UK plc

About the author

Kenneth Lysons is a graduate of three universities and a member of several professional organisations. He has had a long involvement with retirement planning and was for some years secretary and later chairman of the St Helens Preparation for Retirement Committee.

Since his 'retirement' from a senior educational appointment in 1983 he has researched and lectured extensively, particularly in the areas of management and education.

He now works as a freelance writer and consultant and is the author of six previous books and over two hundred published articles.

To Gillian Sarah Lysons

Acknowledgements

No one can write a book without becoming directly or indirectly indebted to many people.

I am particularly grateful for the assistance given by Dave Hitchen of the Department of Social Security; to Anne McGoldrick of Manchester Polytechnic for permission to quote from her paper 'Early Retirement – A New Leisure Opportunity', and to Maggie Smith and her publishers, Lifeskills Associates, Leeds, for the use of the skills analysis exercise in Chapter 2.

Librarians are indispensable to all serious writers. I gladly pay tribute to the help given by the librarians of the Picton Library, Liverpool, the Prescot Branch of Knowsley Library Services, and the St Helens College of Technology.

Eddie Dyja was an unfailing source of support and made many constructive criticisms in the most courteous way. I am also grateful for amendments to the text suggested by Caroline Hartnell.

Finally, I must once more pay tribute to the work of my assistant, Jeanne Ashton, for help with the research and for her skill in deciphering my handwriting and typing most of the book. The remainder of the typescript was undertaken by Alison Gillies.

Kenneth Lysons
January 1992

Introduction

Opportunities do exist for older people to use some of their time to earn money in retirement. Changes in working patterns, earlier retirement and longer life expectancy have all combined to make this more of a possibility than it has ever been before.

Working patterns were turned on their head during the 1980s with the micro-electronics revolution, the decline in traditional industries, high levels of unemployment, and, finally, recession. Through voluntary early retirement, and in some cases compulsory redundancy, more people stopped working before the State Pension age (60 for women and 65 for men). The decade ended with the abolition of the Earnings Rule in October 1989. By making it possible to earn without the State Pension being affected, this opened the door for older people to continue working profitably for as long as they wished.

In addition, people are healthier these days, and live longer. If you are retiring early at, say, 55, you are likely to have a great deal of life ahead of you, on average some 21 and 25 years for men and women respectively. All kinds of opportunities have therefore opened up for older people, including starting a second career, increasing your earning potential by doing some further training, or using your existing skills and experience to set up your own business.

There are also signs that employers are beginning to recognise the value of older workers, who can provide experience, reliability and stability. Age Concern is committed to ensuring that ageism in recruitment comes to an end, and has joined with other organisations to form the Alliance Against Ageism. We already campaign against the constant flow of negative images and prejudices depicted by the media which foster stereotypes of older people and ultimately affect their chances of employment.

At present job advertisements reflect a clear preference for younger workers. This is partly due to ignorance on the part of employers, which has led to a number of common misconceptions about age and ability. Because of such misconceptions many employers refuse to consider applicants purely on age grounds.

Age Concern firmly believes that age as such is unrelated to job performance. Age is rarely a genuine employment requirement. In the USA, Canada and France the law bans the use of age limits in recruitment advertising. In Britain, we should also outlaw this practice and promote the employment of older people, based on their ability – not their age.

While some people over 50 are no longer actively seeking full-time work, many would welcome part-time jobs. Older workers may therefore be suitable for all kinds of part-time work, including short-term assignments or providing cover for absences due to sickness or holidays.

It would, however, be wrong to assume that jobs for older people have to be mundane and involve limited responsibility. Skills and experience are priceless commodities and should not be overlooked – as we have all learned, at one time or another, as a result of working with someone more experienced than ourselves.

Each individual has a right to make choices about when they will retire. People should be entitled to retire whenever they wish, within a broad age band, rather than being constrained by the age limits of 60 and 65. Legislation also needs to be introduced to protect the rights of the older worker, in terms of benefits and concessions.

Earning Money in Retirement is aimed at anyone wishing to supplement their post-retirement income. You may be taking early retirement and wanting to plan ahead. You may be having to accept compulsory redundancy, and feeling anxious about your future prospects. This book points you in the right direction and shows that it is possible to earn money in retirement. The fact that you have retired or are about to retire should not be a barrier. You can succeed if you plan carefully, define your objectives, and adopt a positive attitude.

Sally Greengross
Director
Age Concern England

CHAPTER ONE

You and your retirement

What do I really feel about retirement?

What sort of life will I lead once I have left work?

Do I want to carry on doing some sort of paid work?

How well-off am I likely to be?

Retirement has often been described as the longest holiday of your life, but you may well not be content simply to stay physically and mentally active: you may also feel you want to continue to make a useful contribution to society. Doing some sort of work is a good way of doing this, and of supplementing your income at the same time.

How you adapt to the changes and opportunities presented by retirement will depend on your personal circumstances. This chapter therefore looks at your attitude to retirement, the lifestyle you are likely to adopt, and your motives for working in retirement. Finally, it looks at financial planning – how to work out exactly how well-off you are going to be, and how much extra money you are going to need, if any, to enable you to live the sort of life you are hoping to lead.

Your attitude to retirement

Your feelings about retirement may well change with time and circumstances. Some people who are apprehensive about retirement find it is the happiest time of their lives. Others, who eagerly await it, are disappointed when their expectations are not met.

The following list gives some typical attitudes to retirement. Assuming that you have not yet retired, you might like to consider which of these most nearly expresses your own feelings. If you have already left work, think back to how you felt about retirement before the event, and consider whether you still feel the same way.

Anticipating retirement	Retired
I am looking forward to retirement very much.	I enjoy retirement very much.
I think I am looking forward to retirement.	Retirement is better than working.
I am not sure how I feel.	I am not sure how I feel.
I don't think I am looking forward to retirement.	I would sooner be at work.
I hate the thought of retirement.	I hate retirement.
I don't want to retire.	I don't want to be retired.

How you feel is likely to be influenced by your personal circumstances and your feelings about your pre-retirement job.

Personal circumstances

Your life at home, financial position, health, leisure interests and age will all have a bearing on your attitude to retirement. You are more likely to be looking forward to it if your health is good, your finances are secure, and your home life is happy. You may look forward to spending more time on your hobbies, developing new ones, or even turning them into ways of making money. Equally, you may look forward to spending more time with friends and family.

If things are not going well at home and you feel there will be an enormous gap to be filled when you stop working, you are likely to dread the thought of retirement. In this case, a positive attitude, while not solving your problems, may prevent you feeling old, unwanted, unwell, alone and bored.

Circumstances at work

Retirement will take you away from a working environment where you spent a considerable amount of your time. This may come as a welcome release. The physical and mental demands of your job may have caused stress and anxiety, you may have found the journey to work tiring, you may have felt that you never got proper recognition for the work you did. Worse still, you may have found your job boring and unfulfilling – something you had to do to make ends meet.

On the other hand, you may miss some positive elements related to your job. These could include responsibility, status, making decisions, and the feeling of job satisfaction. You may feel the loss of the security gained through having a steady job with regular pay increases. You may also find you miss things that you have taken for granted, such as the actual office environment, your working habits and even your lunch breaks. Finally, you may miss your working relationships, not just with your close colleagues, but also with all the other people you met during your working life.

The following case histories illustrate the way circumstances influence attitudes to retirement:

Bill works on an assembly line. The job, though highly paid, is only semi-skilled and provides no scope for individual initiative. Noise makes conversation with workmates difficult, except at break-times. Labour turnover is high, so long-term friendships are exceptional. Bill's satisfactions are found away from the job in his home, garden and church, and supporting his local football team. Apart from a substantial reduction in income, he has no regrets about stopping work. He is eagerly looking forward to retirement.

Zareena, manager of a large purchasing department, has decided to accept an offer of early retirement. Initially, she was pleased with her decision, but she has since realised that release from a responsible job will also mean a loss of some of the things she has taken for granted – status, congenial colleagues, a comfortable office, secretarial assistance, scope for decision-making and outside contacts. Zareena is counting the days – but not to retirement; rather she keeps checking how long she has left in the job.

Your lifestyle in retirement

Before retirement you may spend, on average, between 40 and 60 hours a week travelling to and from work and at your place of work. On retirement these hours revert to you.

How you use this time will depend on your lifestyle. Lifestyles clearly differ from person to person but they can be roughly categorised. Anne McGoldrick, in her study of early retired men aged 45–64, identified ten categories of lifestyle adopted by these early retirers. Although her research related to men, the lifestyles she identified also apply to women, so her list has been adapted.

You may like to assess your own personal situation in relation to these categories. If you are about to retire, how do you see yourself spending your time once you have left work? If you have already left, it will be a matter of looking at how you actually spend your time. You may find this useful for planning ahead, as it will help you see how much time you plan to devote, or already devote, to a particular area and to gauge the possibilities for doing more.

Rest and relaxers
Those who follow the more traditional retirement patterns based on reading newspapers, watching TV, listening to the radio, gardening, going on walks, and taking car trips.

Home and family people
Those who value increased time with their families and friends.

Hobbyists
Those who pursue or develop hobbies or interests for which they found insufficient time when at work.

Good timers
Those who use retirement to enhance their social life, by going out in the evenings, travelling, and taking more holidays.

Committee and society people
Those who get fully involved in running clubs or organisations, getting on decision-making committees or helping organise events.

Volunteers
Those who join local community groups or voluntary organisations and help out as volunteers.

Further education people
Those who get involved in further education, whether this means attending a local college course in pursuit of a hobby or taking a degree course at a university.

Part-time jobbers
Those who engage in part-time paid employment, both to fill their time and to supplement their income.

New jobbers
Those who choose a similar job to the one they had previously, or else take a less demanding or stressful full-time job.

Second career people

Those who use early retirement as an opportunity to start an entirely new career, possibly after a period of retraining.

These categories are not of course mutually exclusive. Your retirement lifestyle may be a combination of several. The more time you spend in one area, however, the less you will have available for others. According to Anne McGoldrick, about half the people who reach State Pension age continue in some form of full- or part-time paid work.

Your retirement lifestyle is also likely to change with time. The earlier you retire, the greater emphasis you are likely to place on further education, getting a part-time job, or even starting a second career. As you grow older, you may well want to spend more time just relaxing.

Your motives for working in retirement

Different people have different motives for working in retirement. You may wish to retain the sense of purposefulness, the sense that you are making constructive use of your time, that you had when you were working. You may see retirement as an opportunity to extend yourself and acquire new skills. You may miss the companionship you enjoyed at work. Many, perhaps most, will see earning money as their primary motive, but it is unlikely that this will be your only reason for wanting to carry on working.

Using your time constructively

Pursuing your hobbies and leisure interests is obviously a constructive way of spending time, but you may consider paid work the best way to use some of your time. This need not mean a full-time job, and it may develop from a hobby: you may, for example, find dressmaking or do-it-yourself work enjoyable, and it may also prove profitable if you start offering to do jobs for friends.

Maintaining skills or acquiring new ones

Throughout your working life you will have built up a fund of experience based on skills and knowledge, and it seems a pity to throw all this away once you retire. The best way of maintaining your skills is to continue to use them. The doctor can take on locum work, the plumber occasional jobs, the draughtsman a home-run plan drawing service.

You may also wish to use retirement, especially if you retire early, to acquire new skills or improve existing ones: the home decorator might acquire the professional touch, the executive achieve computer literacy, the typist transfer to word processing. There are plenty of part-time and full-time training courses that will help you achieve your aims (see pp 44–47).

The following are examples of people who have made use of their skills to find new jobs:

Barbara, a former accountant with a legal publishing company, originally joined the Inter-parliamentary Union as a bookkeeper to cover the summer holiday period. Since then she has acquired three further part-time bookkeeping jobs, which virtually fill her week. She is now helping an Indian art gallery, a bespoke tailors and a small publishing company with their accounts.

Charles was a manager in charge of customer relations with a large chain of newsagents and stationers. He has found the perfect part-time job for his retirement: he works for a major food company writing personal replies to customer complaints.

Regaining some of what you liked about work

The discipline of work – rising at a set time, maintaining your appearance, and so on – may be something you want to hold on to in retirement. Work also brings you into day-to-day contact with people, and this may provide a necessary escape from stress or loneliness. You may also cherish the status of having a job, especially if you have felt a loss of identity and significance on ceasing work.

Increasing your income

Even if you have worked out in advance how much money you are likely to need when you retire, and have made adequate financial provision, you may still find you could do with a bit more money – perhaps because you take up a new hobby, or perhaps simply because life proves a bit more expensive than you anticipated.

If you do not have an occupational pension, or your entitlement is small, you may find yourself really struggling to manage on the income you have, and if you retire before the State Pension age (currently 60 for women, 65 for men), you will not even have the cushion of the State Pension.

If for any of these reasons you want to increase your income, you will need to work out your financial position and see how much you really want to earn.

Your financial position

Whether you cease work voluntarily or involuntarily, and irrespective of age, it is a good idea to do some financial planning before you retire.

It is likely that you will have less income in retirement than during your working life, though if you retire at the State Pension age, a combination of occupational and State Pension may mean that there is not too great a gap between your pre- and post-retirement income.

But what really matters is not the gap between your pre- and post-retirement income but the gap between your post-retirement income and expenditure. It is likely that your expenditure, too, will be lower once you have left work, so you may not actually be any worse off, or you may find the gap between your income and your expenditure is smaller than you had feared. Whatever your situation, it is sensible to work out whether your post-retirement income is likely to be sufficient to meet your post-retirement needs – and if not, how large the shortfall is likely to be.

To do this you should first work out how much income you are likely to receive once you have retired from your pension, savings and investments, and benefits. You should then take into account any deductions that may affect your income, such as taxation and National Insurance contributions. Next, you need to calculate your post-retirement expenditure. Having made all these calculations you will be able to see how well-off you are likely to be and whether you will need to earn to sustain the standard of living you want.

Inflation is unpredictable, but as a rule of thumb the value of money is likely to go down. Although some pensions and investments are inflation-linked, salaries and wages are more likely to keep pace with inflation. Because of this it is best to take some account of inflation in your calculations.

The couple in the following example discovered they would be able to manage better than they had expected:

Fred was almost 60 when he was unexpectedly asked to accept early retirement. He discussed the situation with his wife Nancy. Their mortgage, though small, had not been completely paid off. Fred suffered from angina, but had hoped to continue working until he was 65. He recognised, however, that any new job might impose an unacceptable strain on his health.

Although Fred's occupational pension would be increased to the sum he would have received at 65, he was worried about the effect on their standard of living, particularly since they would have to wait five years before he received his State Pension. (Nancy had always paid the married woman's reduced National Insurance contributions, so would not get her married woman's pension until Fred drew his pension.) However, Nancy worked part-time at the local supermarket, and her income, though not substantial, had been put aside in a high-interest building society account.

One evening, some weeks before the retirement date, Fred and Nancy decided to work out how much worse off they would be after making possible economies, and whether in any month they would have cash-flow problems through expenditure exceeding income.

They discovered that by stopping work Fred would make quite significant savings on fares and lunches. Even after making a pessimistic forecast and allowing for inflation, Fred and Nancy found that they could still manage with the money they had and would receive.

Sources of income

Prior to retirement your income includes your salary from work, which is affected by tax, National Insurance contributions, any contributions towards your occupational or personal pension, and any other income such as interest on your current savings or investments. What remains after deductions is the money you actually have to spend, or your spendable income. In retirement, unless you know that you are going to carry on working, your income will come from the following sources.

PENSIONS

Occupational pensions

If you have an occupational pension, this is likely to be your main source of income once you retire. It is therefore important to know exactly how much you will receive and what the payment conditions and arrangements are.

Some employers run separate occupational pension schemes which are 'contracted out' of the State Earnings-Related Pension Scheme (SERPS). 'Contracted out' means that you do not pay for the SERPS provision as part of your National Insurance contribution. The schemes usually provide larger pensions than SERPS, and the longer you work with a company, the bigger your pension will be. You will need to check your entitlement from your pensions officer (the personnel or accounts department should have the details).

There are two types of contracted out occupational scheme: salary-related schemes and money-purchase schemes. Salary-related schemes are normally based on a proportion of final earnings, so it is usually fairly simple to work out how much you will receive. Money-purchase schemes are based on the amount paid by you as contributions. In either case a certain amount can be taken as a lump sum, and the rest will be used to purchase an annuity (a pension of a fixed or increasing amount). You may consider using part of the lump sum for large payments such as paying off your mortgage.

Finding out how your occupational pension will fare against inflation is important when calculating your long-term finances. You should find out if your pension is index-linked. Some pension schemes are designed to keep up with inflation, but more often they simply give an annual increase to help keep up. Others make no such provision at all. As the years pass some pensions may therefore lose their value, particularly if inflation is running high. For those in schemes that do not keep up with inflation, it may be worth making voluntary extra contributions during the last years at work, up to the allowable maximum.

If you are made redundant or are forced to retire early because of ill-health, you are normally given 'added years', that is, the same pension as if you had worked to the usual retirement age. If you voluntarily take early retirement, you will not normally receive an 'enhanced' (added years) pension.

Having established how much your pension is going to be, you should find out how long you will have to wait for the first payment, as well as when and how subsequent payments are to be made.

If you have various pensions preserved in schemes from different former employers, you will have to gather these together. The Occupational Pensions Advisory Service (address on p 114) will be able to help with this and other problems. The Registrar of Pension Schemes at the Occupational Pensions Board can also help trace pensions from previous employers (address on p 115).

Personal pensions
Personal pension schemes are saving plans, run by insurance companies, banks and building societies. You pay in a regular premium which is invested to provide a pension when you retire. Again, you will be able to take a certain amount as a lump sum.

Personal pension schemes are often taken out by self-employed people who would otherwise only receive a State Basic Pension. You can take out a personal pension if you are an employee, but you will have to remain in SERPS unless the pension meets the requirements of 'contracted out' schemes. See pages 103–104 for more information about personal pensions.

State Pensions

Most people receive a Basic Pension from the State. To qualify you must have reached State Pension age (60 for women, 65 for men) and have fulfilled National Insurance contribution conditions. Normally, you need to have satisfied the contribution conditions in your own right, but married women, divorcees or widowed people may be able to claim a pension on their partner's or ex-partner's contributions.

A claim form will be sent to you about four months before you reach State Pension age. If you have not received the form you should contact your local Benefits Agency (social security) office.

You may decide to have your pension paid through a weekly order book which you cash at a post office. Pensions are paid one week in advance. You can also have your pension paid directly into your bank or other savings account, on a four-weekly or quarterly basis.

If you want to retire before State Pension age, ask your local Benefits Agency to check whether your National Insurance record will be enough to give you a full Basic Pension when you reach the qualifying age. You cannot draw your State Pension before then in any circumstances.

If you retire from work because of ill-health, you will receive credits towards your pension. Men between 60 and 65 will also receive credits automatically, as will anyone under 60 who is seeking work, so it may be worth signing on as unemployed even if you are not entitled to benefit. If you find that your contribution record is incomplete and you are not entitled to credits, you may want to consider paying voluntary contributions.

If you have reached State Pension age when you retire, you can choose whether to draw your State Pension (including Additional Pension and Graduated Pension) or defer it in order to gain increases later on. You can defer your pension for up to five years. If you defer your pension, it will be increased by about 7.5 per cent for each full year that you defer it – about 37.5 per cent over the full five years. Any week that you draw Sickness or Invalidity Benefit or Unemployment Benefit will not count towards extra pension.

You will need to work out whether it is better for you to draw your pension or defer it. As pensions are taxable, it may well be better to defer it if you are still working and earning a reasonable amount. On the other hand, since the abolition of the Earnings Rule, it is possible to draw your State Pension and go on working, as your pension is no longer reduced or stopped if your earnings are over a certain limit.

The *Additional Pension,* which started in 1978, is based on earnings on which you have paid contributions. You can ask your local Benefits Agency office for a statement of your Additional Pension and an estimate of what you can expect when you retire.

Graduated Pension existed from April 1961 to April 1975 and was based on graduated contributions paid from earnings. Again, if you qualify for this pension you should ask the Benefits Agency for details. For further information about the State Pension, see Age Concern England's book *Your Rights* (details on p 129).

SAVINGS AND INVESTMENTS

Another source of income will be interest on your savings and money coming from premiums from investments.

You should look at the savings you have accumulated over the years and consider whether you intend to continue saving at the same rate, and whether you are investing your savings in the best way for your particular needs. Consider whether you want to be able to draw on your savings for short-term needs, and find out if your money is easy to draw out and whether you need to give any notice. You may feel it is a good idea to have some money set aside for an emergency and want to put this money in a bank or building society account.

Investments come in many forms such as stocks and shares, unit trusts and personal equity plans. Investments always involve an element of risk, since you can lose as well as gain money, but you will want to be sure your investments are as safe as possible. You should also find out about the regularity of interest payments, or dividends. As with your savings, you will need to assess whether you need regular payments to supplement your income. For further information and advice see *Your Taxes and Savings*, published by Age Concern England (details on p 129).

STATE BENEFITS

Depending on your circumstances you may be eligible for some State benefits. For instance, if you are on a low income or have to retire early due to ill-health you may qualify for certain benefits. These should be taken into account when you are assessing your full financial position.

Income-related benefits

If you are on a low income, *Income Support* provides help with basic living expenses. *Housing Benefit* and *Community Charge Benefit* provide help with rent and with meeting part of the cost of the Community Charge (which may become the Council Tax) respectively. The *Social Fund* provides lump-sum payments to meet exceptional expenses like funerals and heating during cold weather.

Benefits for disabled people and their carers

If you have been unable to work for at least 28 weeks through illness, you will be eligible for *Invalidity Benefit*. Once you reach pension age, you can choose whether to draw your State Pension or to continue to receive Invalidity Benefit for the next five years. The advantage of the latter is that it is not taxable. On the other hand, there are earnings limits for Invalidity Benefit but not for the State Pension.

If you are severely disabled and need frequent attention, supervision or to have someone watching over you, you will be eligible for *Attendance Allowance*. If you become unable to walk or have great difficulty in walking due to physical disablement before the age of 65, you will qualify for *Mobility Allowance,* but you must apply before your 66th birthday.

Finally, if you are under pension age and unable to work full-time because you are caring for a severely disabled person for at least 35 hours a week, you will qualify for *Invalid Care Allowance*. Once you reach State Pension age, the allowance will be stopped if the pension you receive is more than the allowance. If you are not entitled to a pension, you can carry on receiving Invalid Care Allowance provided you still qualify on other grounds.

Where eligibility for a benefit depends on being below pension age, this means at present that men qualify for five extra years. However, this may be changed in the future, as under European law the age limits should be the same for men and women.

Because the benefits schemes are often complex, the Department of Social Security (DSS) is taking a different approach with the Benefits Agency, the new DSS administrative agency. It aims to provide more information, an increased emphasis on the quality of service, and more links with community groups such as Age Concern and Citizens Advice Bureaux through 500 offices nationwide.

If you think you might be eligible for any of these benefits, contact your local Benefits Agency office. Full details about benefits are provided in Age Concern England's *Your Rights* (details on p 129).

Deductions from your income

Deductions from your pre-retirement income will include income tax, National Insurance contributions, contributions towards your occupational or personal pension, and maybe trade union fees. When you retire, some but not all of these deductions will cease. It is therefore important that you should be aware of your position, particularly in relation to taxation and National Insurance contributions.

TAXATION

Taxation does not go away in retirement. Any earnings from work, State Pension, occupational pension and most investment income will still be taxable – though many of the State benefits mentioned above are tax-free.

Everyone is entitled to a personal tax allowance, which reduces the amount of income on which tax is paid. Whether you are married or single, this allowance increases once you reach the age of 65, and there is a further increase when you are 75. However, if your total income is over a certain limit, the higher allowance will be reduced gradually, according to how much over the limit you are, until the basic personal allowance is reached.

If you want to find out whether your income is likely to be taxed, you will need to contact the tax office that handles your affairs. If you are still in paid work, this will be your employer's tax office; if you are self-employed, this will be the office covering your business; if you are unemployed or retired, this will be your last employer's tax office. Tax offices and enquiry centres are listed in the phone book under 'Inland Revenue – Taxes, HM Inspectors of'.

Further information about taxes is available in Age Concern England's *Your Taxes and Savings* (details on p 129).

NATIONAL INSURANCE

Once you reach State Pension age you will not have to pay National Insurance contributions even if you are still working. You should receive a certificate of exemption from the DSS to give to your employer, who will still have to pay contributions for you.

If you are under State Pension age, whether you are liable to pay contributions basically depends on how much you earn. If you are an employee, you will be exempt from payment of contributions if your gross earnings from any one employer are below what is termed the 'lower earnings limit', which corresponds roughly with the flat-rate pension for a single person. So if you work for several employers but earn less than the limit from each, you will be able to keep more of your gross income than if you earned the same amount from one employer. If you are self-employed, you will not have to pay contributions if your profits are below a certain limit. But if you do not pay contributions those years will not count towards your State Pension.

For further information about National Insurance see Age Concern England's *Your Rights* (details on p 129).

Your expenditure

If you have not yet retired, the easiest way to work out your post-retirement expenditure is to see how much you are spending now, and where your patterns of expenditure are likely to be different in the future. The 'Annual Expenditure' table below will give you an idea of the kind of items you will need to consider. The two columns are for your pre-retirement and post-retirement expenditure. You will thus need to work out, for each item, whether you are likely to spend more or less once you have left your job. If you have already retired, you will obviously only need to fill in the 'Current' column.

Completing the table will reveal certain facts. The first is that your main savings are likely to be in areas previously associated with employment. These include the cost of travelling to work, parking, meals out and clothes.

Some items such as repairs and maintenance of property might, in a particular year, be less than estimated. However, it is sensible to allow for the full amount and even deposit any surplus in a building society account. Any repairs that need doing should be done sooner rather than when the costs are higher; if you do have any surplus over the year, it might be wise to devote it to this purpose.

ANNUAL EXPENDITURE

	Current	Projected
Gas		
Electricity		
Other power		
Water		
Telephone		
Community Charge		
Mortgage/rent		

Maintenance and decoration of property _____ _____

Estimated repairs _____ _____

Household insurance _____ _____

Food _____ _____

Tobacco/alcohol/sweets _____ _____

Household goods and services _____ _____

Clothing and footwear _____ _____

Personal goods and services _____ _____

Presents/donations _____ _____

Union/professional subscriptions _____ _____

Car maintenance _____ _____

Petrol _____ _____

MOT Test _____ _____

Annual road tax _____ _____

Annual car insurance _____ _____

AA/RAC subscription _____ _____

Fares/season ticket _____ _____

Leisure goods/services _____ _____

Holidays _____ _____

TV licence/TV rental _____ _____

Life assurance premiums _____ _____

Bank charges _____ _____

Savings _____ _____

Miscellaneous _____ _____

Total _____ _____

How much do you need to earn?

You are now in a position to make the final calculation that will reveal whether you do need to earn in order to supplement your income. This is a simple comparison of your post-retirement spendable income (ie the money you have coming in, minus any deductions) with your expenditure. If what you have coming in is less than your projected expenditure, you will need either to earn some money in order to bridge the gap or to think about modifying your lifestyle in some way.

MODIFYING YOUR LIFESTYLE

Your standard of living may need modifying rather than lowering when you retire. You might, for example, prefer staying at home to holidaying abroad, and public transport to the strain of driving. You might also consider moving to a smaller house.

The habit of economising wherever possible by taking advantage of available concessions is something you will probably develop naturally. Find out if there are concessionary bus fares for pensioners in your area, or special concessions for services or leisure activities. The cost of a Senior Railcard can often be recovered by the savings made on one journey, and out-of-season rates can reduce the cost of holidays. At home, doing jobs yourself which previously you would not have had time to do can save money. You can also, paradoxically, save by spending. For instance, it is more economical to buy rather than rent a television.

Now that you have had a good look at your financial position, and at what you are hoping to get out of retirement, you are in a good position to decide whether or not you want to do some paid work. Even if there does seem to be a gap between your post-retirement income and expenditure, you may decide not to do any work to supplement your income. You may feel you would rather reduce your expenditure in some way than give up any of the precious leisure time you have been so eagerly looking forward to – perhaps to pursue some hobby which you have never really had time for before.

If, however, you do decide to do some paid work, you will now need to consider what sort of work you would like to do. Your immediate feeling may be that you do not have much to offer a prospective employer. The next chapter looks at your skills, knowledge, hobbies and interests, and any other assets you possess that might be useful in earning money.

CHAPTER TWO

What have you got to offer?

Have I got any skills or experience that are likely to be of value to a prospective employer?

Could any of my hobbies be turned into ways of making money?

Has my home or any of my other possessions any earning potential?

What about getting more training?

When you first ask yourself the question 'What do I have to offer?' you will probably think of the skills associated with your pre-retirement job. If you do not particularly want to continue doing the same job, or even working in the same field, you may feel you are at a dead end.

But in order to answer this question properly, you need to take a far broader look at yourself and what you can do. Even in your job you will probably have picked up many valuable skills besides those most directly related to the job. The very fact that you have had so much experience may itself be of value to a prospective employer. Alternatively, you might have a hobby or interest with earning potential, or be able to put your home or other possessions to some money-making use. Finally, you might be able to combine with others to provide products or services, or you could go on a training course, either to acquire completely new skills or to brush up on existing ones. When considering what you might be able to do to earn money, it is vital to look at all the possibilities.

What special skills or knowledge have you got?

When considering this question, your mind will naturally turn to your pre-retirement job. An electrician will think of house wiring and electrical repairs; a secretary of shorthand, typing and word processing; a teacher of imparting and assessing knowledge. These are all skills related to specific tasks. Often the work people take on in retirement is directly related to their pre-retirement job, as in the following examples:

Kate *retired from her post as an accounts clerk and decided to offer a bookkeeping service to small businesses. She advertised in the local press using a box number and began working for three traders. She later bought a computer and, as a result of recommendations, her clientele has increased to six, to whom she offers a complete range of office services, including wages preparation.*

Peter worked as a driver for a large company. When he retired he contacted a number of firms that provided cars for weddings and offered to work part-time as a driver. He soon had no shortage of engagements. His employers welcomed his ready availability and the fact that they could use him according to their requirements.

But you may also have skills and knowledge that you have never recognised as having earning potential. Whatever your job, you are likely to have acquired certain general skills, such as the ability to solve problems and to communicate and interact with other people, which are vital for almost all occupations. In addition, a good head for figures, a familiarity with computers, and the ability to speak another language, while not necessary for all occupations, are becoming increasingly useful.

Some skills are acquired mainly through experience. The ability to cope with non-routine situations or emergencies, knowing who to contact or where to get information, an awareness of time-saving methods or procedures, the ability to evaluate information – all these are gained largely through experience and will enhance whatever other skills you possess. Because of this, many people have found that the very fact that they are so experienced can be a valuable asset when looking for ways to earn in retirement.

It might, therefore, be a combination of general skills, rather than a skill related to a specific task, that will provide you with the means of earning money when you retire.

Maggie Smith, in her excellent pre-retirement book *Branching Out* (see p 125), has devised a useful exercise in skills analysis. The following list, based on her exercise, categorises skills under the headings 'Data', 'People', 'Things' and 'Ideas'. The aim of the list is to help you make a complete assessment of what you have to offer. The idea is that the various items will act as triggers, to which you might respond 'Yes, I am good at that'. If you go right through the list, putting a tick by each of the skills you feel you possess to any degree, you may well be surprised at how many different skills you do have, often in areas you had not previously thought of.

DATA

- [ ] Analysing, dissecting – sorting and sifting information or things
- [ ] Calculating, computing
- [ ] Diagnosing – looking for problems
- [ ] Examining – observing, surveying – an eye for detail and accuracy
- [ ] Following instructions, diagrams, blueprints
- [ ] Managing money – small or large sums
- [ ] Manipulating numbers rapidly – mental arithmetic

- [ ] Memorising numbers and facts
- [ ] Organising, classifying
- [ ] Problem-solving
- [ ] Reading – to extract facts
- [ ] Report-writing
- [ ] Research – gathering information
- [ ] Reviewing, evaluating
- [ ] Taking an inventory
- [ ] Other areas in this group

PEOPLE

- [ ] Conveying warmth and caring
- [ ] Drawing people out
- [ ] Giving credit to others, showing appreciation

- [ ] Helping others
- [ ] Initiating relationships
- [ ] Leading, directing others
- [ ] Listening

- [ ] Motivating people
- [ ] Organising people
- [ ] Performing – in a group or on stage
- [ ] Promoting change

- [ ] Selling, persuading, negotiating
- [ ] Showing sensitivity to others' feelings
- [ ] Teaching, training
- [ ] Other areas in this group

THINGS

- [ ] Assembling things
- [ ] Building, constructing
- [ ] Driving – car, motorbike, etc
- [ ] Finding out how things work
- [ ] Fixing, repairing things
- [ ] Growing things
- [ ] Hand-eye co-ordination
- [ ] Handling things with precision, speed
- [ ] Keeping physically fit

- [ ] Manual dexterity
- [ ] Muscular co-ordination
- [ ] Physical strength
- [ ] Quick physical reactions
- [ ] Tending animals (sensitivity skills apply here too)
- [ ] Using hand tools
- [ ] Using machine, power tools
- [ ] Using technology – typewriter, computer, etc
- [ ] Other areas in this group

IDEAS

- [ ] Composing music
- [ ] Conveying feelings or thoughts – through body, face or voice
- [ ] Conveying feelings or thoughts – through drawing, painting, etc
- [ ] Designing – things, events, learning materials
- [ ] Developing others' ideas
- [ ] Fashioning or shaping things or materials
- [ ] Having insight, using intuition
- [ ] Improvising, adapting
- [ ] Innovating – creating, seeing alternatives
- [ ] Reading for ideas
- [ ] Sizing up situations or people quickly
- [ ] Working creatively – colours, shapes, faces
- [ ] Writing creatively
- [ ] Other areas in this group

To some extent the usefulness of this exercise will depend on your age. The earlier you retire, the more feasible it will be to develop new skills or use your existing skills in a fresh context. In some areas, eg accounting and secretarial work, skills in computing and word processing, if not already acquired, will be essential if you are to enhance your opportunities of earning in retirement.

Another exercise that might be useful in helping you build up a more complete picture of what you can do is to make a list of all the different occupations you have ever had experience of, on a paid or unpaid basis. You will need to cast your mind over all the different areas and stages of your life – the various jobs you have done; any voluntary work you have undertaken; your domestic activities, hobbies and leisure interests. You will probably end up with a fairly mixed list, with perhaps such diverse items as mending televisions, book-keeping, translating, cake decorating and growing flowers.

The next stage is to ask yourself the following questions about the areas in which you have had experience:

- Where did you gain your experience? (Experience with a prestigious employer can help you get work.)
- How varied is your experience?
- Over how long did you gain the experience?
- Was there anything special about that experience, ie did you carry out unusual tasks, work on a particular project, etc?
- What did you learn from the experience?
- Is the experience still relevant to employment needs?
- Is the experience only relevant to a specific job or occupation, or could you make use of it in a variety of different situations?
- What can you offer as a result of your experience, eg anything that a young person could not provide?
- What employers might be interested in your experience, or could you make use of it as a self-employed person?
- How can you bring your experience to the notice of potential employers or users?

Have you got hobbies with earning potential?

Hobbies and interests can be expensive. But they can also be profitable. Even if you do not actually earn money through a hobby, it can be a means of saving money. Growing fruit and vegetables, making toys for your grandchildren, and doing your own decorating are just a few examples of hobbies that can save money.

But hobbies can also be developed into lucrative full- or part-time activities. Just to take the examples given above, you might start selling the fruit and vegetables you grow, or making toys for other people's children or grandchildren, or doing decorating for other people. If you do have a hobby that you enjoy, developing it in this way could be an ideal way of earning money in retirement – unless you are absolutely forced to, you should avoid taking on work that does not interest you.

The following are two examples of people who have set up profitable businesses based on what were previously spare-time interests:

Desmond, *always a lover of books, with a fine personal library, has built up a postal bookselling business specialising in biographies and works on the Second World War. He began by storing books in his garage. He enjoys buying up collections; some of the books find their way into his own library, but these acquisitions are more than paid for by the sale proceeds from other items.*

Julia *has turned an interest in research into a profitable one-woman business. Her work involves researching and writing histories of commercial buildings and private homes; these usually run to 12–15 pages, plus maps and illustrations.*

If you do succeed in tranforming a spare-time activity into a time-consuming and money-making business, you may even find that you need to take up some new hobby to provide relaxation from it. If you have plenty of other interests already, this will of course present no problem.

Have you got possessions with earning potential?

Consider the earning potential of your most basic possession – your home. If you live by the sea or in the country you could provide bed and breakfast. Your kitchen offers all sorts of possibilities – bottling, cooking, sweet-making and sandwich-making are just a few. A spare-room can become a work-room for dressmaking, knitting, secretarial work or writing. Another possibility is desk-top publishing. Sometimes referred to as personal publishing, this may be defined as the ability to disseminate words and pictures from a single desk-top. If you are a skilled operator, it offers lucrative possibilities for earning in retirement, as the woman in the following example discovered:

Ann, on retirement, bought a word processor which she installed in her spare-room. At first she undertook straightforward assignments such as typing up cvs and author's manuscripts. Later she invested in a desk-top publishing package and she is now able to produce a wide range of leaflets, brochures, newsletters and local histories equal in quality to those produced by professional publishing operations.

Your earning potential will be further enhanced if you can also provide writing and publicity services.

There are a number of legal matters to consider if you do propose to use your home in any of these ways. These are dealt with on pages 59–60.

Land, too, has enormous potential: you could grow flowers or vegetables, breed livestock, or even provide parking facilities. Your garage could be let, or used by a skilled car mechanic to offer repair services.

Hiring equipment

You do not necessarily have to own the equipment you put to money-making use. Equipment can be hired. Community resources such as the reference section of your local library are freely available to everyone. You may, because of your training or previous employment, have access to restricted resources, as do the people in the following examples:

John lives midway between the two universities of which he is a graduate. As a graduate he is entitled to use the university libraries. He also has access to a number of specialised professional libraries. He uses these resources to research material for use in the articles he produces as a freelance writer.

Mary made an agreement with her employers that she could continue to use the photocopying equipment of her late firm at a low rate after she retired. She has now established a part-time secretarial bureau, and finds this facility extremely useful.

You might even get ideas about equipment to hire from browsing through the *Yellow Pages*. The list of possible equipment is, of course, infinite. But do check the cost.

It is often a good idea to hire an item of equipment initially, even if you are thinking of buying it. You may regard the purchase of an item of equipment as an investment, but before tying up your capital in this way, you should first do some research to make sure there is sufficient demand for your intended use.

Have you got time to sell?

All employment involves the buying and selling of time, but selling time is used here in the restricted sense of providing cover, being at a certain place for an agreed time-span so that someone else can be released for other activities, eg lunch breaks. You may or may not be expected to undertake other simple, routine tasks such as non-specialist nursing, retail selling or simple reception duties during the period for which you provide cover. There is certainly a demand for people who can, at short notice, undertake cleaning, shop-minding or security work. Some of these vacancies may be advertised in your local Job Shop, in the local newspaper, or even in shop windows.

Child-minding while parents are at work or looking after old or invalid people for a number of hours weekly is another area for which part-time help is in demand. If child-minding appeals to you, you should register with your local social services department, who will first ensure that you can provide adequate care and facilities. Other sources of useful information, including advice on fees, include the National Childminding Association and the Pre-School Playgroups Association (addresses on pp 120, 115).

The social services department and the appropriate voluntary bodies, including your local Age Concern group or Old People's Welfare

Council, should be approached if you are interested in providing care for elderly people.

General advice and help for all carers is given by the Carers' National Association (address on p 120).

Home-sitting and invigilating examinations are two other ways of selling time. Home-sitting means looking after someone else's home while they are away. Although you do have responsibilities, it can be almost a paid holiday. You are usually paid a weekly amount, plus travelling expenses. For details of openings contact Homesitters Ltd or Universal Aunts (addresses on pp 114, 115).

Examination invigilation involves supervising people who are taking examinations to ensure that the regulations of the examination bodies are complied with and that those sitting the examinations do not cheat. For openings, contact your local education office or the examination officers of professional bodies. A full list of such bodies is given in *British Qualifications,* available in most reference libraries (see p 124).

Could you combine with others to provide products or services?

You might find the idea of setting up a business on your own too daunting, but like the idea of doing so with other people. In addition, you might like the companionship, particularly if you live alone.

A good example of what can be done here is that of a 72-year-old man who, with five other retired draughtsmen, established a drawing office. Each man worked three days a week but the office was open all week. They were soon inundated with work, and with good reason. They were punctual, their technical knowledge and skill were excellent, and there was never any trouble about overtime. In the first year their numbers increased from six to sixteen. The men not only enjoyed the extra money, but they all said that their general health and mental outlook improved significantly. The only rule was that no one under 65 could be employed.

This idea has unlimited applications. Similar groups could be formed by people in almost any occupation.

There are advantages and disadvantages in combining with others to earn in retirement. The advantages include the pooling of responsibility, knowledge, skills, expertise, equipment and capital; cover during holidays or sickness, and membership of a working group. The disadvantage is some loss of independence, since the group rather than you yourself determines working arrangements. There can also be legal disadvantages. The group may, in law, be a partnership, so that the members become severally and individually liable for any debts incurred by the undertaking while they are partners.

In general, such groups should be kept small so that the participants can work together on a basis of mutual trust and confidence. It is also advisable that the authority and responsibilities of participants should be set out in a written agreement.

What about further training?

Training, prior to or after retirement, can open up numerous possibilities. It can equip you for a complete change of occupation, by providing you with new skills or knowledge, or it can be used to brush up on skills you already possess. Training may be full- or part-time; you can attend a college or other institution, or take advantage of the opportunities offered by distance or open learning (see pp 46–47).

A change of direction

If you intend to retire early, it might be possible to train for an entirely new occupation while you are still doing your pre-retirement job. The following provides a good example:

John, an engineer, had a desire to enter the stipendiary ministry of the Anglican Church. His bishop suggested a three-year course of part-time training, which John began when he was 45. He completed the course successfully. At the age of 50, he gladly accepted an offer of early retirement so that he could enter his new vocation.

About 14 centres offer part-time training for the Anglican ministry, most of which also cater for candidates from non-conformist denominations. You can obtain details from your local priest or minister or by writing to the Vocation Adviser at the Advisory Board of Ministry (address on p 113).

If you are a Catholic, your parish priest will be able to direct you to the vocation director for the diocese, or you can write to the House of Studies for Late Vocations (address on p 114).

Teaching, particularly in areas such as business and computer studies, mathematics, technology and the sciences, is another possibility. It is useful, and in some cases essential, to obtain a formal teaching qualification. You can sometimes obtain one while holding a teaching appointment. For more information see *Training and Retraining to Teach Priority Subjects*, obtainable from the Department of Education and Science (address on p 114).

Government training

You will be eligible for Employment Training (ET) if you are under 60 and have been signing on as unemployed for at least 26 weeks. You may also be eligible if you want training in certain skill-shortage jobs, are disabled, are leaving the Forces, want to start your own business, or have been away from work for at least two years because of family commitments.

ET aims to help you find out about the current labour market, build your confidence and job-hunting abilities, introduce you to new technology, give you new skills, or provide training to help you start a business on your own.

From April 1992, responsibility for all government-funded training will be undertaken by the 82 Training and Enterprise Councils (TECs) which are being established throughout the country. It is understood that they will give priority to providing training or retraining for people wishing to re-enter industry or commerce, including 'women returners' and people who have retired early.

For the address and phone number of your local TEC and details of what training is available phone 0800 444246.

Full-time higher education courses

If you retire early you might want to take the opportunity to increase your earning potential by taking a degree or other higher award. For information about what courses are available see *Second Chances*, an annual guide to adult education and training opportunities (details on p 126).

You may be eligible for a local education authority (LEA) grant or award. Some grants are mandatory, ie LEAs are required by law to pay them. Others are discretionary, ie whether you receive one will depend on the LEA decision. For more information about grants see *Student Grants and Loans*, a brief guide obtainable from your LEA.

Further education

Colleges of further education and evening institutes offer a wide variety of part-time day or evening courses. Some are 'non- examination' but many lead to recognised qualifications, such as those of the City and Guilds of London Institute (CGLI) whose address is on page 114. Typical CGLI courses include Caring for Children, Hairdressing, Micro-computers, Painting and Decorating, and Photography.

The *Directory of Pre-Retirement Courses* (see p 125) could be a useful source of ideas. It lists 200 courses in Great Britain and Northern Ireland, offered by voluntary, public sector and commercial organisations, and ranging from a day to a term in length.

Open learning and distance learning

'Open learning' is a term covering all arrangements intended to overcome restrictions on access to knowledge and education, including the need for particular educational qualifications.

'Distance learning' refers more specifically to the removal of geographical restrictions: teachers and taught are separated geographically but may communicate with each other by post, radio, television or electronic mail. It is also possible to study at home, using a learning package devised by a specialist publisher of distance learning material, such as the National Extension College or the Open College (addresses on pp 115, 119), and, in addition, to have access to special equipment such as computers, electronic typewriters and laboratories.

'Open learning' also implies flexibility as regards the content and duration of courses. It thus gives you the opportunity to decide what you will learn, where you will learn it, and over what period of time.

The Open University is often seen as the epitome of distance learning. In addition to its degree courses, it offers a Continuing Education Programme of short vocational and general interest courses or study packs. Successful completion of some of these courses leads to a certificate or diploma that may be credited towards an Open University degree. Details can be obtained from the Open University Central Enquiries Office (address on p 115).

The Open College was set up in 1987 to provide flexible vocational training for both organisations and individuals. In addition to publishing open learning materials, it offers student and trainer support through a number of centres. As with the Open University, most of the Open College courses are supported by radio and television broadcasts.

The *Directory of Open Learning Opportunities*, published by the Training, Enterprise and Education Directorate (address on p 115) and available at most libraries, tells you where you can get advice on choosing appropriate courses and support while doing them, including access to computers and libraries.

You should by now have a fairly clear picture of what you have to offer a prospective employer, and of what resources you have available if you want to set up a business of your own. You may have decided, having considered all the possibilities, that you want a complete change of direction, or that the skills you possess are not sufficient to enable you to do what you want. In this case you may well have decided to undertake some sort of further training. If you are not opting for training, you are now ready to address some other extremely important questions about your post-retirement working life: Do you want to work for someone else or for yourself? How much time do you want to devote to working? You might also want to consider the possibility of working from home.

CHAPTER THREE

Working: When, where and for whom?

Do I want to work for an employer again?

Do I want to work part-time or full-time?

Can I earn the extra money I need if I work part-time?

Could I cope with being self-employed?

What do I feel about working from home?

Finding the answers to the questions set out on the previous page – probably the main questions you now need to ask yourself – may not be a straightforward matter, and may in the end involve something of a balancing act. You may feel you would ideally like to work only a couple of mornings a week. After all, the very word 'retirement' will be a misnomer if you spend all your time working. Retirement should be a time for 'work, rest and play', with work providing variety and perhaps the financial wherewithal to enjoy rest and play more fully. On the other hand, having assessed your financial position (see pp 20–31), you may realise that you really want to earn more money than you can possibly earn in two mornings a week.

Deciding whether you want to work for someone else or for yourself may be equally difficult. If you have worked for someone else all your life, you may well relish the thought of being your own boss at last, making your own decisions and working the hours that suit you. On the other hand, you may feel you would miss the relative security of being employed, and you are aware that running your own business can involve a lot of worry and long hours of work. The considerations are endless.

Working for someone else

If you are wondering whether you really want to go on working for someone else, and are feeling attracted by the idea of working for yourself, it is worth considering the advantages you would lose if you ceased to be an employee and decided to start up your own business:

- Reasonable security
- No risk to personal savings or other capital
- Shorter hours
- Regular holidays
- Regular income
- Payment of wages during sickness

- Payment for overtime
- More limited responsibility
- Less planning of future work
- Less worry outside business hours
- Companionship of your fellow employees

You should also bear in mind that the advantages of working for yourself may not be as great as they appear at first: having more freedom of action and being your own boss can in practice mean a lot of worry and hard work.

Assuming that you do decide to go on working for someone else, you will need to consider carefully how much time you want to devote to earning before rushing to apply for jobs. Do you want to work part-time or full-time? Because the majority of people who earn money in retirement choose not to work full-time, part-time work seems a good place to start.

Part-time work

Employers have traditionally employed part-time staff:

- where the job does not warrant a full-time employee, eg in catering, clerical and secretarial work;
- where there is a need to increase flexibility of service, eg in building societies and banks, and shops with late-night or Saturday opening;
- where it is necessary to provide cover for existing staff, eg at meal breaks, in the evenings or at weekends.

If a valued and experienced employee is unable to continue to work full-time, employers will sometimes keep them on a part-time basis rather than lose them altogether, as in the following example:

Paul worked as a plumber with a company offering a 24-hour emergency service. Good, reliable plumbers are not easy to come by, so when he was approaching retirement he was asked if he would stay on and work two eight-hour shifts. Paul agreed, provided he did not have to work any nights.

So if you enjoy your job and are approaching retirement, it is always worth asking your employers if they would be interested in employing you part-time.

From the retired person's standpoint, part-time work (whether as an employee or working for yourself) has several advantages, in addition to increasing your income:

- It may smooth your transition from full-time employment to retirement.
- It will help you to remain part of the community and maintain contacts.
- It will provide some of the discipline of working.
- It can provide variety in your life, especially if you have more than one part-time job.
- It may lead to a full-time job – if you want it.
- It will help you maintain your skills and feel you are using your time in a worthwhile way.

It is often assumed that part-time staff are paid at a lower rate than full-timers, but this is in fact unusual. Similarly, staff benefits and training are often identical for full-time and part-time staff, though the latter do face some discrimination in relation to job security and redundancy payments. The European Community has, however, published a directive stating that 'steps must be taken to prevent discrimination' against part-time workers.

There are a number of books on part-time work available. One of the best of these is *Part-Time Work* by Judith Humphries (see p 126).

Full-time work

It can, of course, be objected that 'full-time work in retirement' is a contradiction in terms, since if you are working full-time, you can hardly be retired.

But there are circumstances in which you might think about full-time work. First, you might have reached retirement age and be asked to 'stay on' by your employer because your skills and experience are still needed. Alternatively, you might have taken early retirement but still like the idea of having a full-time job. If you are contemplating a full-time job, there are some basic questions you should put to yourself:

- Why do you want to work full-time, ie for money or for companionship?
- What kind of job do you want? Clearly you are not looking for a job that will last a lifetime, so you can be more flexible over the type of work you do.
- What can you offer? Here, you might find it useful to look at the skills analysis exercise on pages 36–38.

You should also consider the disadvantages of taking a full-time job. These include loss of time, which would otherwise have been yours to spend as you wished, and loss of status – it is unlikely that you will get a job with the same level of responsibility as your pre-retirement employment.

If you do decide to carry on working full-time after retirement from a previous job, you will probably find it most satisfying if your new job provides a complete change of direction, as with the example of John given on page 44.

Job-sharing

Job-sharing is an arrangement by which two or more people share the hours, duties, pay and benefits of one full-time job. It therefore provides a kind of half-way house between full- and part-time work. With the agreement of their employers, job-sharers can divide their time in a number of ways: one can work mornings, the other afternoons; they can split the week, one working Monday to Wednesday lunchtime, the other working Wednesday lunchtime to Friday, or they can work alternate weeks.

An increasing number of organisations are setting up job-sharing schemes. The most important reason for doing so seems to be to retain staff, including older employees. If, like the woman in the following example, you are on the verge of retirement, but would like to continue to work part-time, it might be worth suggesting job-sharing to your employer, who might not have considered this approach. One problem for employers could be having to pay two lots of National Insurance.

Sheila was a children's clothes buyer in a large department store. Six months before she retired, she approached her employer and said she would like to carry on working part-time, possibly on a job-sharing basis. Her job has now been split into two: she buys for the 0–5 age range and her job-sharer deals with the 6–10 range.

Job-sharing may also enable employers to implement phased retirement schemes according to which, in the last two years of service, the number of days worked by employees is progressively reduced from five to four to three days, thus cushioning the sudden shock of retirement. The opportunities for job-sharing appear to be greatest in administrative, clerical and secretarial work, nursing and retail distribution. Professional work, including journalism, law and medicine, also offers possibilities.

How much time do you want to spend working?

Having considered all the different options, you should now be in a better position to decide how much time you want to spend working. The following questionnaire is intended to help you reach a decision. Because the issue of how much you want to earn is inseparable from that of how many hours you want to work, questions about how much you want to earn are included.

1 Do you wish to work

☐ Full-time   ☐ Part-time

2 If part-time, how many hours per week do you wish to work?

☐ More than 16   ☐ 8–16

3 On how many days a week are you willing to work?

   1   2   3   4   5   6   7

4 On what days, if any, are you not prepared to work?

   Mon   Tue   Wed   Thur   Fri   Sat   Sun

5 Do you prefer to work

   ☐ Mornings only   ☐ Afternoons only   ☐ Either

6 Are you prepared to work evenings?

   ☐ Yes   ☐ No

   Are you prepared to work shifts?

   ☐ Yes   ☐ No

7 Are there any periods in the year when you would not wish to work?

   ┌───┐
   │   │
   └───┘

8 What is the net amount you wish to earn, ie after tax, NI contributions, travelling and other expenses?

   Per week   Per annum

   ┌──────────────┐   ┌──────────────┐
   │ £   │   │ £   │
   └──────────────┘   └──────────────┘

9 What is the minimum hourly rate you would accept for your work?

   ┌──────────────┐
   │ £   │
   └──────────────┘

Completion of the questionnaire will enable you to prepare for yourself a statement of what, ideally, you would like to do, similar to the following:

```
Part-time work required for not more
than 8 hours a week, preferably on
Monday and Tuesday mornings, throughout
the year except July. Minimum acceptable
hourly pay £4.50, or £36 weekly.
```

Having arrived at such a statement, you should bear in mind that it is only an ideal. In practice, you will have to be flexible, so the statement should act as a guide and not a rule. Flexibility and availability are two factors that make retired people attractive to employers. The more rigid you are about hours, days, times and pay, the more difficult it will be to get a post-retirement job. The general pattern of part-time employment for pensioners is either two or three whole days where travelling is involved, or half-days for a local job.

Working for yourself

Many people who have worked for someone else all their lives dream of starting up on their own. The offer of early retirement at the age of 55 or so can give you the opportunity to turn this dream into reality. You should have the cushion of an occupational pension, and if you receive a gratuity from your employer, this, combined with your savings, should provide useful capital.

If you have been made redundant, your redundancy payment may also give you sufficient capital to start a business. Remember, too, that setting up on your own need not require a lot of capital, so if you are unemployed or simply like the idea of a change, it is always worth considering.

If you are thinking of starting your own business, you may well be attracted by the idea of having greater freedom of action and no one to tell you what to do. But your greater freedom could prove illusory if the pressures involved in starting a business and keeping it going force you to work longer hours than you intended. You may also like the idea of increased reward for effort, but this too could prove illusory. To begin with, at least, you may well find that your income is lower than before. And if you face some sort of setback, you may have to put in a lot of work simply to put things right. By contrast, working for someone else will give you more limited responsibility and the security of a regular income.

On the other hand, the fact that you can choose to retire when you like is a definite advantage, as is having a business to sell when you finally retire (with considerable Capital Gains Tax relief for older owners) or to pass on to your heirs on your death.

There are also some other factors you should consider, particularly if you are thinking of running a full-time business.

Your age
For how long will you want the business? Remember you have only a limited number of years to achieve success.

Your health and that of your spouse
Remember that, when self-employed, you cannot afford to be ill.

Your temperament
Can you cope with decision-making and uncertainty without undue stress? Remember that when self-employed, you cannot resign. You are the boss! Are you likely to feel lonely and isolated working on your own?

Your family
Are they behind you? Remember, a full-time business means that they will have to accept long hours, often no weekends, and few holidays in place of the leisure companionship and absence of worry usually associated with retirement.

Your knowledge and experience
This may easily be dated. Remember that in a technological age, it is necessary to run very hard even to stand still.

Your expected return
Will this compensate you for all the risk, effort and worry involved? Remember that the personal capital committed, if suitably invested, could provide a certain risk-free return without any effort on your part.

One further consideration is whether the proposed business could easily and profitably be disposed of should you die.

Working from home

For someone wishing to earn in retirement, working from home has obvious advantages:

- You have flexibility in choosing when and what hours to work.
- You avoid travelling.
- Some expenditure, such as heating and lighting, may be allowable against tax if you are self-employed (see pp 101–103).
- It may be possible to involve your family in your work.

There are, however, some disadvantages. Working from home can be lonely, and you may find it hard to cope with the distracting claims of family, housework and paid work. Considerably more self-discipline is required when you work at home than on an employer's premises.

The Department of Employment defines a 'homeworker' as 'someone who works in or from the home for an employer or contractor who supplies work and is responsible for marketing and selling the results'. Many people, however, work from home on their own account. A number, for example, are already engaged in information technology (IT) homeworking. This means using a fax machine, a phone with answering machine, and/or other aids to speedy communication such as a personal computer with a modem. The latter uses the telephone line to send messages from your computer screen, via systems such as Telecom Gold, to another user with similar equipment. By these means, you can set up a business communications centre anywhere, no matter how far away you are from a large town or even your customers. The number of people working in this way may increase substantially among workers who organise and apply information.

Employees working from home may be lent IT equipment. Such workers usually have exceptional skills that are not easily replaceable, and the assignments are often temporary, for example during maternity leave or shortly before or after retirement.

Dress machinists and workers with similar skills are often wanted in towns. The goods are delivered and picked up again, but this type of homeworking often tends to be unregulated. In general, unless there are pressing reasons for doing so, and an appreciative employer, working as an employee at home is usually underrated and under-paid. When considering the possibilities of working from home, some of which are touched on in Chapter 5, you should also bear in mind certain legal complications.

The legal position

The legal restrictions that do exist will not normally affect people wishing to earn in retirement, but should at least be mentioned.

Check your lease if you are a tenant, or your deeds if you are an owner occupier, to ensure there are no covenants restricting the use of your house. If you have a mortgage, this should not be affected so long as the primary use of the house continues to be residential and not business. If, however, your house is primarily used for commercial purposes, the Mortgage Interest Tax Relief given on the house will be affected. On the other hand, if you take out a loan to buy a property which you let, the interest on it will be allowable for tax purposes as a deduction from your letting income.

If you regularly work from home and this involves a 'material change of use' of the premises from a 'private dwelling', you must obtain planning permission from the planning department of your local authority. Whether something amounts to a material change of use will be determined by the specific circumstances. If you use your spare room as a study or for clock repairs, you will not need planning permission. If, on the other hand, you convert your front room into an office and advertise your services as a financial consultant in the window, the planning authority may decide there has been a material change of use. Planning permission is unlikely to be required if:

- you use your house mainly as a home;
- you do not use large parts of your house exclusively for paid work;

- your work does not cause a noticeable increase in the amount of traffic or the number of people calling at your house;
- your activities are not too conspicuous. Teaching people to play drums might bring you to the attention of the local authority, whereas monthly bridge lessons in your home would not.

You should also check your insurance. Your normal household contents policy may not protect you against the loss of the more valuable business items, eg a word processor, so you may need to make special arrangements. If in doubt, check with your insurance company.

What to avoid

Retired people without special skills or expertise may be attracted by advertisements offering work assembling or packing items such as crackers or Christmas cards. These are the 'traditional' forms of homeworking, infamous for low pay and poor working conditions. The Manchester Low Pay Unit Information Pack issued in 1990 relates how a woman in Tameside making Christmas crackers earned just over 2p per cracker and had to make 70 crackers an hour to earn £1.50. In another case, a woman earned £1.08 an hour from sewing cushion covers, out of which she had to pay for heating her room and running her sewing machine. Clearly, this is not earning in retirement, but sweated labour. If you see advertisements asking you to send money for directories of homework opportunities or lists of potential employers, or as a token of goodwill or an 'agency fee', remember Mr Punch's advice to those about to marry and DON'T.

If you have decided how much you want to earn, what sort of work you might be interested in doing, how much time you ideally want to spend working, and whether you want to work for yourself or someone else, you have now made all the preliminary decisions youneed to make about earning in retirement.

If you have come to the conclusion that you would like to work for yourself, it is time to get started. Chapter 5 looks at the various options for starting up your own business, from running a bed and breakfast establishment or buying a Kentucky Fried Chicken franchise to setting up as a consultant or a self-employed dressmaker. It also looks at the sort of help that is available, and your tax position as a self-employed person. If you feel you would prefer to work for someone else, it is time to think about getting a job. How to set about doing this is the subject of the next chapter.

CHAPTER FOUR

Working for someone else

Where do I look for a job?

How do I set about preparing a cv?

Will I be able to cope with an interview after all these years?

Going through the whole process of searching for a job and then applying for it may seem pretty daunting – particularly if it is a long time since you last had to do it. This chapter goes through the whole procedure, stage by stage, starting with looking for a job and going on to drawing up a cv and preparing yourself for an interview.

Where to look for a job

If you have decided that you would like a post-retirement job, it is no good simply hoping that something will turn up, because you will probably have to wait a long while. If you actively look for a job, you are much more likely to find one.

There are seven main sources from which post-retirement employment may be sought:

- Job centres
- Your present employer
- Networks
- Employment agencies
- Advertised vacancies
- Self-advertising
- Canvassing prospective employers

Job centres

Before job centres were set up, unemployed workers registered at a benefit office for whatever unemployment benefit they were entitled to, then went to another agency to look for job vacancies. Today, job centres fulfil both roles: as an unemployment benefit office and as a government-sponsored employment agency. They advise claimants not only on their benefits but also on how to get back to work and how to write a cv, and they will arrange interviews if you see a suitable job advertised in the centre. Sometimes, particularly with the long-term unemployed, job centres will organise training courses, with travelling expenses paid and a guaranteed interview at the end.

Job centres will register you as looking for work. When you register you will have to give details of your occupation. If any suitable vacancy occurs, you will be notified. If, however, a vacancy occurs outside your stated occupation, you will not be told. You should, therefore, give careful consideration to how you wish to be registered, and possibly put yourself down as available for two or three types of work.

Job centres also work on a self-service basis. The basic details of vacancies are given on typed cards displayed around the walls. If you see a suitable job, fuller details will be given at the counter.

Your present employer

Your present employer might be glad to retain your knowledge and expertise on a part-time basis, temporarily, permanently or as a resource to cover emergencies such as holidays, sickness or rush periods. Sometimes, as suggested earlier (see pp 53–54), two former employees can continue to cover one full-time post on a job-sharing basis.

Often your employer will not have considered offering you post-retirement employment because it is assumed you would not be interested. It is a good idea, therefore, to enquire about the possibility of part-time employment well before you leave and a successor is appointed. When doing so, stress the advantages for your employer of retaining your services. These include savings in recruitment costs and retaining someone of proven competence, integrity and reliability.

Networks

'Networking' refers to the use of contacts to obtain advice, information and jobs. The 'old boy system', clubs and professional associations are examples of networks. Less formally, your network may include your family, neighbours, and the friends and acquaintances you have acquired through your church, your job, membership of societies, evening classes or trade union, or your local pub, as in the following example:

Maria was employed cooking directors' lunches for a large city firm. A few months before she retired, she was having a drink with friends in the local pub when the publican mentioned that he was thinking of branching out and offering lunches for coach parties a couple of days a week. Maria said that she might be interested in doing the catering – which she now does every Wednesday and Saturday.

Through all these sources you can let it be known that you are ready, able and willing to work. The significance of networks is reflected in the fact that only about half of all available jobs are ever advertised.

If you do have friends or acquaintances who you think might be able to offer you work, avoid putting them in the difficult situation of having to say 'No' to a direct request for work. Instead, broach the subject obliquely by asking for their advice regarding possible employers who could use your skills. Everyone likes to be thought an expert and most people like to help. By asking for ideas, especially about people you might approach, you avoid embarrassment on both sides. The essence of using networks to find work is summed up in the advice 'Circulate and communicate'.

Employment agencies

Apart from the many agencies listed under 'Employment Agencies' or 'Personnel Consultants' in the *Yellow Pages*, there are a number of organisations that specialise in finding jobs for retired or older people.

Some local Age Concern groups have established their own employment bureaux, as have some Pre-Retirement Associations. A pioneer in this field was the Glasgow Pre-Retirement Association (now the Scottish Retirement Council). Sadly, their employment bureau has recently been closed. A full list of local Pre-Retirement Associations and Councils is obtainable from the Pre-Retirement Association of Great Britain and Northern Ireland (address on p 115). Some Citizens

Advice Bureaux have also established 'Over Sixty' employment bureaux.

Probably the most famous employment agency for older people is *Success After Sixty*; others are *Age Works* and *Buretire*. All three handle vacancies in any field at any level, permanent or temporary, full-time or part-time. The feeling that the skills and experience of older people should not be wasted is central to their operation. The addresses of these and the other employment agencies referred to in this section are on pages 116-117.

Some other agencies are more specialised in their area of work. *Executive Standby*, for example, places retired executives in management or similar posts with industrial, commercial or voluntary organisations. They also employ executives and 'contract hire' them to the organisation with a vacancy. Normally, the upper age limit is 60.

Most professional associations, such as the British Medical Association, the Law Society and most of the accountancy bodies, keep registers of members available for employment. If you are a member of any professional association, it is worth enquiring whether it keeps a register of members seeking employment. Some of the trade unions provide similar facilities.

A number of agencies exist specifically to find jobs for ex-service personnel. The *Officers' Association* helps anyone who has held a commission in HM Forces, including the Territorial Army. The age limit tends to be 65 in London and 60 elsewhere. The *Regular Forces Employment Association* helps anyone who has served in the non-commissioned ranks for a minimum of three years. It has 40 branches throughout the country. The *Corps of Commissionaires* is not an employment agency as such, but offers employment to coastguards, firemen, merchant seamen, police and prison officers as well as ex-service personnel. Age limits are approximately 60 and 70 for permanent and temporary work respectively. There are branches of the Corps in most major cities. The *Royal British Legion Attendants Co*

Ltd offers full- or part-time work as car park attendants, commissionaires and security guards to ex-service men and women.

Advertised vacancies

These appear in local newspapers, the 'quality' daily and Sunday papers, and even in shop windows. You can also consult specific papers such as the *Times Educational Supplement* and trade or professional journals. Details of relevant publications can be obtained from the Classified Index of *Willings Press Guide*, which should be available in your local reference library. This gives details of all professional, trade, technical, scientific, religious and industrial journals in the United Kingdom, ranging from accountancy to zoology.

Self-advertising

Instead of looking for advertised vacancies in the local and national press or elsewhere, you can make use of the same channels to notify employers that you are willing and able to take on work. Taking the initiative in this way can be very successful. With press advertising you can, of course, preserve your anonymity by using a box number. Shop windows are especially useful if you are offering child-care, or electrical repairs, cleaning and similar services.

Canvassing prospective employers

Another method of self-advertising is to write to prospective employers telling them what you can offer. A curriculum vitae or cv (see pp 72–77), suitably presented, will often make a better impression than simply writing a letter. Directories of local employers, available in your local reference library, will provide suitable addresses. Alternatively, you can look through the *Yellow Pages*. You could make a few telephone calls to 'test the water'. Otherwise, duplicate a number of letters and send them off.

Combatting ageism

Your opportunities of getting a post-retirement job may partly depend on your being able to counter certain negative misconceptions about the potential of older people held by many employers.

In a perceptive paper presented to the House of Commons Committee on the Employment of the Over 50s in 1989, the employment agency Success After Sixty stated that the main obstacle facing people in this age group who are looking for jobs is employer ignorance.

If you are over 50, you will often be seen as having one foot more or less in the grave. It is assumed that your health will be poor and your capability decreasing, that you will be slower than a younger person, and that you will not want to work beneath a less experienced, less qualified supervisor. Due to such stereotypes, many employers refuse to consider some applicants purely on age grounds, without considering what they have to offer, or else they offer ridiculously low salaries.

Another misconception relates to older people's skills. According to the House of Commons Committee, 'part of the stereotype which causes discrimination by employers is that the over 50s have out-of-date skills, are too inflexible to learn new ones or are too old to make investment in new learning worthwhile'. This attitude overlooks the fact that, in many occupations, ten years is as long as any training will be useful. Providing training for someone of 55 will, therefore, often be as worthwhile as giving it to someone of 25.

In the USA the Age Discrimination in Employment Act of 1967 aims to prevent discrimination by making ability rather than age the criterion for employment. Similar legislation for the United Kingdom has been resisted partly on the grounds that compulsory retirement at a given age may be essential to safeguard employment and promotional opportunities for younger people.

In the absence of legislation against ageism, it may be up to you to counter the negative stereotypes of older workers if you want to get a job. As well as pointing out the falsity of such views, it is important to emphasise the positive aspects of age, including:

- A lifetime of experience.
- Ready availability.
- Reliability, proven ability and punctuality.
- Lack of career aspirations.
- Retired people can be useful for short-term assignments or to cover absences due to sickness or holidays.
- They can also be employed where the work does not occupy a whole working day, or is not continuous.
- Most older people mix well and are surprisingly adaptable.

Another important fact that needs stressing is that there is as much variation in ability among the young as among the old. In many jobs older workers may perform more effectively than the young.

A number of key facts about age and employment are listed in a Statement on Age and Employment issued by the Institute of Personnel Management (IPM), and these may well provide you with useful ammunition when talking to a prospective employer:

- Age is a poor predictor of job performance.
- It is misleading to equate physical and mental ability with age.
- A greater number of the population are living active, healthy lives as they get older.
- There is an increasing number of older workers in the labour market.
- Age is rarely a genuine employment requirement.

The following quotation, taken from the IPM statement, might also be useful in helping to counter employers' prejudices:

> The efficient and effective use of people's skills requires that employment decisions should be based on competencies, qualifications, skills, potential and objective job related criteria obtained through the careful analysis of job requirements and satisfactory job performance.

The use of age bands, age guides and age related criteria reduces objectivity in employment decision-making. It increases the likelihood of poor quality and inappropriate decisions which are harmful to individuals and wasteful of people's skills.

Reading such authoritative statements on the value of older workers will also be good for your own self-confidence and self-esteem: it is vital that you should feel confident of your own worth in the face of the negative stereotypes you are likely to encounter.

Applying for a job

Once you have heard of a suitable vacancy, you should do some simple research before deciding whether you wish to apply. If you have to apply for an application form, further details of the vacancy will sometimes be sent with the form. It is, however, rare for job descriptions to be prepared for a part-time job unless the job is at a fairly senior level. If no details of the job are sent, try to obtain answers to the following questions:

- What will I be required to do?
- What hours will I be expected to work?
- Is overtime customary or likely?
- Is any travelling involved?
- What will I be paid?
- Is any training involved?
- For how long is the job likely to last?
- Why did the previous job-holder leave?

Sometimes you will be invited to apply for a job by telephone. If you telephone about a vacancy, you are well advised to remember the following hints:

- If possible, telephone from home or a friend's house. If you do have to use a phone box, use a phone card or ensure you have a plentiful supply of 10p pieces.

- State clearly why you are telephoning, eg 'I am telephoning about the vacancy for a part-time clerk advertised in today's issue of the *Star*.'
- Try to find out from the person who answers the phone the name of the person who is dealing with the vacancy, so you can approach them by name, eg 'Is that Miss Smithers? I am telephoning about the vacancy . . .'
- Before telephoning make a list of all the questions to which you would like answers before applying for the job.

Usually, however, you will have to apply for a job by post. If so, the matters to which you should now turn your attention are your cv, the covering letter, and how to prepare for an interview.

Your cv

Your cv, or curriculum vitae, is your personal advertisement. It should give a brief account of your education, qualifications and previous employment.

PREPARING YOUR CV

When preparing your cv, think carefully about the type of work you want. Decide on what occupational title best fits the skills, knowledge and experience you can offer to an employer. Next, take two or three sheets of paper and write down the following headings, leaving about half a page between each: Personal Details, Employment History, Special Experience or Abilities, Education and Qualifications, Other Information.

Under Personal Details write down your date of birth and marital status.

Under Employment History detail the jobs you have had, *working backwards*, ie giving your last job first. Use three columns to provide the following information: dates of starting and leaving each job (state years only); name and address and business of employer; your job title. You may wish to leave out some of your early employment history if it does not seem relevant or if you have had a great many jobs.

Under Special Experience or Abilities reflect on each job you have held and write down:

- what the employer did;
- the size of the employer, ie number of plants, number of people employed;
- the title of the person to whom you were directly responsible;
- your wages or salary;
- the number of people you supervised (if any);
- the types of equipment you used;
- your responsibilities;
- promotions achieved;
- your achievements, eg problems you encountered and how you overcame them.

You will obviously not include all this information in the final cv, but it is helpful to gather it all together at this stage and you can then decide what is relevant.

Under Education and Qualifications, again use three columns to assemble information relating to: dates of starting and leaving; name(s) of educational institutions attended (start with your secondary school); qualifications obtained at each institution, stating class or distinction where applicable and scholarships, honours, awards achieved. However, if you have higher educational qualifications, it may not be necessary to include the lower school qualifications.

Under Other Information write down any items that you think will help an employer to form an estimate of you as a person, eg hobbies, voluntary activities, proficiency in languages, overseas travel (if extensive), publications, etc.

CHOOSING REFEREES

You should also think of possible referees. Normally two will be sufficient. Think carefully about what information the referee will be asked to provide and his or her credentials for doing so.

Generally, a prospective employer is interested in three things: your ability to do the job; whether you will be able to integrate into an existing workforce, and your character. Information on the first and second of these is best provided by a former employer; the third, character, may be vouched for by a clergyman, bank manager or some other person of standing who has known you over a considerable period of time.

In choosing referees, ask yourself:

- What kind of information do I want this referee to provide?
- For how long has the referee known me?
- What standing will the referee have in the eyes of a prospective employer (the more senior or better qualified the referee, the more weight will be given to the reference provided)?

Remember that it is courteous to approach referees for permission to use their names before doing so.

If your referees are likely to impress a prospective employer, by all means mention them in your cv. Otherwise, make a note of names, titles, addresses and telephone numbers so you can supply these details, if required, without delay.

HOW TO PRESENT YOUR CV

How you present your cv is almost as important as what is in it. Make sure it is typed; if you do this on a word processor, information can be easily added or deleted. Further, any number of copies can be produced, each looking like a top copy. Use good quality, white A4 paper.

Do pay attention to the physical appearance of your cv. Layout, centring, headings, margins, paragraphing, punctuation, spacing and spelling all contribute to its effectiveness as your personal advertisement. Use short sentences and paragraphs. Paragraphs should have double or triple spaces between them. Use underlining and upper-case letters for emphasis.

The information assembled at the preparation stage can be arranged in a variety of different ways. A typical cv format is shown on page 76.

The covering letter

Your cv should be accompanied by a covering letter. This has three objectives: to introduce you to the reader, to indicate what you want to do, and to request a reply.

Your covering letter should be brief. You do not need to include personal details, since these are covered in your cv. But it must be positively written, so that you come over as an achiever. Whenever possible, address it to a specific person. Do ensure that all spellings, especially of names, are checked, and correct titles used.

A typical letter of application is shown on page 77. If it is typed on a word processor, it is easy to insert any number of different addresses and amend the date. This enables you to contact a number of prospective employers, either at once or at different times, without having to write a separate letter each time.

If you are applying for an advertised vacancy, it is a good idea to insert a suitable introductory paragraph, similar to the following:

```
I wish to apply for the part-time post
of progress chaser advertised in the
Barchester Reporter dated 13 February.
```

It is usually advisable to state the type of work you are prepared to accept. In the specimen letter on page 77, the writer, by specifying 'progress chasing, stores control or other related activity', makes it clear that he is not looking for a post similar in status to his pre-retirement job, although the insertion of 'purchasing' leaves this option open.

Curriculum Vitae of
KENNETH GORDON YATES

PERSONAL DETAILS

Born 4.8.1925

Married

423 Lathom Road, Barchester, Barsetshire BA17 6JA

082-426 7255

EMPLOYMENT HISTORY

DATES	EMPLOYER	POSITION HELD
1975-89 (Retirement)	Allington, Barset & Ribchester Local Authorities Purchasing Consortium	Chief Procurement Officer
1969-75	Barset Area Health Authority	Head of Purchasing
1950-69	Atlas Construction Company	Chief Buyer
1941-43	World-Wide Construction Ltd	Clerk in Buying Department

SPECIAL EXPERIENCE OR ABILITIES

(i) In last post responsible for an annual spend of £126,000,000 and approximately 50 purchasing, stores and clerical staff. Installed a complete computerised purchasing and stores system.

(i) Experience of procurement in both the public and private sectors.

EDUCATION AND QUALIFICATIONS

DATES	INSTITUTIONS	QUALIFICATIONS OBTAINED
1935-41	Hallgate Grammar School	School Certificate in 8 subjects. Prefect 1939-41
1947-49	Barset College of Technology - Evening Study	Ordinary National Certificate in Commerce with Credit
1949-51	Ribchester Polytechnic	Purchasing Officers Associations Diploma Associate 1951. Fellow 1972

OTHER INFORMATION

Hon Treasurer, Barchester Council of Social Service.
Member of Barchester Rotary Club.
Fluent German.
Occasional contributor to British and American 'purchase journals'.

REFERENCES AND FURTHER INFORMATION ON REQUEST

```
                          K G YATES
                          423 Lathom Road
                          Barchester
                          BA17 6JA
                          Tel: 082-426 7255


The Chief Purchasing Officer
The Sovereign Engineering Company
Industrial Park
Barchester
BA20 8SA


Dear Sir
I have recently retired at a senior
level after some 40 years' experience
in private and public sector
purchasing.

I wish to obtain a part-time or
temporary full-time post in
purchasing, progress chasing, stores
control or other related activity.

Details of my career are given in the
attached cv.

I am certain I can offer you excellent
service, and would be willing to
attend for an interview at any
mutually convenient time.

Yours faithfully
```

The interview

It may be many years since you were last interviewed for a job. Some reminders about how to prepare for the interview and how to be at your best on the day may, therefore, be useful.

PREPARING FOR YOUR INTERVIEW

Your preparation will mainly consist of gathering background information and thinking about questions you may be asked. It is also a good idea to find out how to get there, if you do not already know.

Background information

Gain all the information you can prior to your interview on such matters as:

- what your prospective employer makes or does;
- how long the business has been established;
- whether it is linked to any other company;
- how many people it employs;
- who the main customers or clients are;
- who its main competitors are;
- what sort of reputation the business has as an employer and among others in the same field.

Such information can be obtained from people you know who are already working for the prospective employer or their competitors, or from the Department of Employment, trade directories, or, in the case of a public company, the *Stock Exchange Year Book,* which you will find in your local reference library.

You may be asked at your interview what rate of pay you expect for the job, particularly for casual or temporary work, so it is well to be informed about the 'going rate' for the job you are applying for. See page 81 for how to obtain such information.

Questions you may be asked

Earlier in this chapter reference was made to the misconceptions held by some employers regarding older people. Suggestions were made as to how you might counter such stereotypes, particularly by emphasising the advantages a retired person can offer an employer.

It is therefore likely that you will be asked questions relating to your age, such as:

- What is your health like?
- Why should we give you the job instead of a younger person?
- How do you think you would get along with younger people?
- Do you think you could adapt to holding a less senior post?
- Why did you accept early retirement?
- What job were you doing before you retired?
- What have you done to keep up to date?
- For how long do you expect to work before you retire altogether?

More general questions often asked at employment interviews include:

- Why do you want this job?
- Why did you stay so long in your last job?
- To whom and for what were you responsible in your last job?
- How would you . . . (technical or other questions testing your job knowledge)?
- What are your leisure interests?
- What payment would you expect?
- When would you be available to start?
- Have you any questions you would like to ask me/us?

The last question can sometimes cause difficulty. The golden rule here is only to ask questions you really need to ask. Do not waste everyone's time by asking questions that are trivial or irrelevant. It is useful, if you have not already been told, to ask: 'How did this vacancy arise?' and 'How soon shall I hear from you?' If you feel you must ask a question and are really stuck, you can always ask to be told more about the job.

How to get there

If the company is situated locally, you will know where to go. If travelling is involved, it may be useful to do a dummy run to find out exactly where it is and how long it takes to get there. If the journey takes too long it might in any case be unsuitable for a retirement job.

PERFORMING WELL ON THE DAY

At the interview itself, how you present yourself is almost as important as what you say. If you want to appear to your best advantage, you should bear in mind the following:

- Be punctual – if you are unavoidably delayed, try to telephone and explain the reason and when you are likely to arrive.

- Be presentable – wear appropriate clothes; you should be neat, clean, tidy and comfortable.

- Be courteous but not servile – regard the interview as a discussion between equals. The prospective employer is not yet your 'boss'.

- Remember the importance of body language – your walk, posture and handshake all convey information about yourself. Avoid gestures likely to irritate or antagonise the interviewer such as lolling back in your chair, placing your hand over your mouth while speaking, avoiding eye contact, or regarding the interviewer with a fixed stare.

- Listen to questions and think before speaking.

- Do not talk yourself out of the job. Answer questions concisely and clearly.

- Learn to control your nerves. Remember that the interviewer is also a human being with hopes, fears and problems like yourself. Learn to relax; take deep breaths to calm down. Make sure you are comfortable in your seat, and remember that if you have prepared for the interview, there is nothing really to worry about.

Do not be overly disappointed if you do not get the first job you apply for. A better one may be round the corner. Contacts are always helpful, so do keep up with groups, clubs, associations – you could hear something to your advantage.

Conditions of employment

Pay

For casual or temporary work you may have to accept what you are offered or forgo the job. But, as already mentioned, you may sometimes be asked at your interview what wages you expect. In both cases a knowledge of the 'going rate' for broadly similar work will prevent you being exploited or asking for too much.

You can obtain information about current wage rates from several sources:

- the annual *New Earnings Survey,* issued by the Department of Employment, available in large reference libraries (this is always very out of date, so you will need to add increases for inflation);
- job advertisements for similar work;
- employment agencies;
- trade unions.

You can also make informal enquiries of people working for the same employer or in the same occupation.

Rates for some occupations such as working in a shop, café or hairdressers, where there is no strong employee representation, are covered by Wage Councils. The employer must post notices informing employees of the agreed Wage Council rates. Homeworkers must be treated no less favourably than their counterparts in a factory or other establishment. Wage Council rates are often available from the Department of Employment's Wages Inspectorate (address on p 114).

The Employer Protection (Consolidation) Act 1978 requires your employer to provide regular itemised statements showing your gross and net wages, variable and fixed deductions, and any variations.

Your rights as an employee

Your statutory employment rights are affected both by how many hours a week you work and by the length of time you have worked for your employer. As far as guaranteed pay (guaranteed minimum payments for days on which your employer does not provide any work), redundancy pay and protection against unfair dismissal are concerned, you have no statutory rights at all if you work less than 8 hours a week. If you work 8–15 hours, you obtain full statutory rights after five years, and if you work 16 or more hours you obtain these rights after two years.

Pay policy is determined by the company, but the law on racial and sexual discrimination and equal pay applies to all workers, full- or part-time.

Benefits you may be offered

Employee benefits are numerous and may include canteen services or luncheon vouchers, company cars, company shops, holidays, assistance with housing, medical services including chiropody, private medical insurance, payment of professional subscriptions, pensions, and recreational or welfare facilities.

Some of these, such as canteen services and recreational facilities, are likely to be open to part-time employees. Access to others, eg pension funds or private medical insurance, is restricted. Many employers take the statutory 16 hours a week threshold, which triggers a number of rights after two years' service, as the starting point for offering non-statutory benefits to part-timers. Other employers use minimum earnings as a basis for determining eligibility. Some exclude part-timers from certain benefits altogether.

Your tax position

Taxation is a large subject. There are, however, several aspects of tax relating to earnings in retirement that you should consider.

As mentioned on pages 27–28, normally all your income, including that from retirement earnings, is assessable for tax purposes. Your income will include your salary or wages, any bonuses, commission or other income from employment, any pensions you have, income from your savings and investments, and any fees or charges for casual work.

Remember that the higher personal allowance for people aged 65 or over will be reduced if your income exceeds a certain limit. Any pension or investment income that you have already paid tax on will be 'grossed up' (to the pre-tax amount) in order to calculate whether you have exceeded the income limit.

If you take a part-time job it is your responsibility, not your employer's, to inform the local tax office, even if you think you are unlikely to be taxed.

Because your net earnings, ie earnings after allowable expenses have been deducted, are taxable (check the current tax level) it is possible that in certain circumstances you would benefit very little from working.

Allowable expenses do not include the cost of travelling to your place of employment. If your travel costs to and from work are high, and you have significant other expenses associated with working, you may conclude that earning money in retirement is not worthwhile. If you are only planning to work a few hours a week, these expenses may seem to absorb a very large part of your income. If you then have to deduct tax, you may feel that what is left is simply not worth having.

CHAPTER FIVE

Working for yourself

What sort of business do I want to have?

Should I buy up an existing business, or is it best to start from scratch?

How much should I charge?

Where can I go for some advice?

If, despite all the possible disadvantages and difficulties, you decide you do want to set up on your own, you still have a great many decisions to make. What exactly do you want to do? 'Setting up your own business' can encompass anything from doing a bit of dressmaking or decorating for friends and neighbours to running a shop full-time or working as a management consultant. Do you want to start from scratch or buy up an existing business?

Once you have decided what you want to do, you will have to think about the practicalities of actually starting up your own business. Knowing what help is available is vital here. If you are offering some sort of service, you will have to decide how much to charge. All these issues are covered in this chapter.

If you want to set up some sort of business that will involve substantial capital outlay, eg on premises, equipment or stock, there are two alternative ways of doing this: buying an existing business or 'starting from scratch'.

Starting from scratch

The exact nature of the business you decide to start will depend on your own inclinations. Many of us have had idyllic day-dreams of forsaking the rat-race to run a bed and breakfast establishment at the seaside or be self-sufficient on a smallholding.

The reality is often different from what we imagine. Bed and breakfast accommodation must yield a sufficient income during the 'season', which is usually quite short, to enable you to live in the much longer 'out-of-season' period when business is likely to be slack. In seaside resorts, competition is likely to be fierce. As for smallholdings, you will find that the work is hard, subject to many hazards ranging from crop-failure and animal diseases to storms and vandalism, and may provide a living at little more than subsistence level.

For an older person, one obvious disadvantage of starting from scratch is that it may take a considerable time for a business to become viable. Another disadvantage is that unless you have had some experience of the relevant activity, you will not have much idea about the demand for the product or service you are offering. It may not in any case be possible to start from scratch – with a sub-post office or pub, for example.

There are, however, obvious advantages in starting from scratch. You will be exploiting knowledge, experience and contacts you have built up yourself. You will not run the risk of being 'taken in' by someone wishing to dispose of a business for dubious reasons. You may also require less capital, since intangible assets like 'goodwill' (see p 90) are not involved. Finally, you can more easily control your commitment in terms of time given to the business.

In general, the more personalised the product or service you are selling, the more likely it is that you will decide to start from scratch.

Buying an existing business

Making preliminary enquiries

You have to be extremely careful when buying an existing business. Whatever the nature of the enterprise, there are some preliminary questions you ought to ask when considering doing so. Here is a checklist:

- When was it established and by whom?
- How many subsequent owners has it had? Why did they sell?
- What are the annual profits? Are these audited? Is the profit trend increasing or decreasing? What are the reasons for this?
- Are the premises freehold or leasehold? If leasehold, how long has the lease to run? Can it be renewed?
- What condition are the premises in? Will much renovation be required?
- Are equipment, fixtures and fittings in good condition? Who owns them?

- What is the condition of stocks? Are they new or obsolete, shop-soiled or deteriorated?
- Are suppliers dependable? Are any agreements due for renewal?
- What is the present and likely future competition?
- What is the location like? Is the business near to schools, bus-stops, railway stations, post offices, etc? Are traffic routes or parking facilities likely to change?
- Why does the present owner wish to sell? Are the reasons given the true ones?
- What is the general reputation of the business in the locality? To what extent does this depend on the personality of the present owner?
- Are the present staff efficient and willing to stay on?
- How does the business, in its existing condition and from the standpoint of potential, compare with others that are available?

Usually, answers to the above are best obtained indirectly. A visit to the locality and judicious questioning of tradespeople or people you meet in cafés, libraries or even in the street will enable you to put together a picture of the business and its prospects and evaluate the answers given by the person who is selling it.

You can ascertain what businesses of the type you want are available through a business transfer agency, which will appear in your local *Yellow Pages*. You should also look at the appropriate trade journal.

The negotiating stage

When you get to the stage of serious negotiation, it is wise to seek the professional services of an accountant or bank manager. But this does not absolve you from doing some homework, particularly with regard to the valuation put on the business you are thinking of buying.

Briefly, the price you will be asked to pay will be determined by four factors: profits, fixed assets, current assets and 'intangibles'.

PROFITS

Treat the profits claimed with some care:

- Try to look at bank deposit or income tax statements over, say, the last three years, rather than the business books.

- Look at the trend of profits. An average figure will not show whether profits are increasing or declining, yet a business with steadily increasing profits will obviously be worth more than one where profits are declining.

- Look at the ratio of profits to sales. An accountant should be able to tell you how the profits–sales ratio for a particular business compares with the average for similar businesses.

- Examine the expenses of the business, particularly wages and rent. The purpose here is to see whether expenses are reasonable.

FIXED ASSETS

These are assets such as premises, fixtures, equipment and machinery. You should find out whether depreciation and obsolescence have been allowed for, and how much the assets are insured for. Remember that items like cash registers, office equipment and shelving may have little value on the second-hand market.

You should also establish how the premises have been maintained. What repairs or renovations will be needed in the next few years?

CURRENT ASSETS

The most important current assets are debtors and stock.

Debtors
You need to know the period of credit granted, what percentage default, and whether provision for this has been made in the valuation. What is the cash flow like?

Stock
You should only be interested in stock that meets current demand and is not 'dead'. An important figure that your accountant should

consider is the rate of stock turnover. Rapidity of stock turnover obviously has a bearing on profits, and it also indicates how well the stock carried meets customer requirements.

INTANGIBLES

The most important intangible is 'goodwill'. Goodwill is the value of the connections of an established business, 'the probability that the old customers will resort to the old places'.The value of goodwill is usually calculated in relation to average net profits. You must also remember that goodwill is only of value as long as the business is a 'going concern'. It is worth nothing if a business is discontinued.

All these factors are important for anyone buying a business. If you are buying a business in your 50s, however, they assume even greater significance, because your working life is unlikely to be long enough to enable you to recoup any serious loss.

What to avoid

You do not have to be a cynic to recognise that there is no shortage of sharks and charlatans purveying 'business opportunities'. Be especially wary of the following.

Partnership propositions
Remember that as a partner you would be liable for all the debts of the firm – your partners' as well as your own – contracted while a partner. Supposedly profitable businesses needing additional funds may be deceptive frauds. Only enter into partnerships with people you have known for a long time and can trust.

Patents and inventions
At best, investments in new inventions or patents are highly risky speculations, at worst frauds.

Job-investments
Here an advertiser offers work on condition that you pay an agreed amount for 'know-how' or the right to participate in his business.

Large earnings and bonuses may be promised to those who invest in the business, but such promises may be fraudulent.

Buy–back contracts
Here a promoter offers to buy back a business if you have not achieved a stated return after one or two years of operating. Like money-back guarantees, such promises are no better than the guarantors and may be worthless.

If someone offers you the opportunity of investing in an enterprise that will bring you high profits for little work, be suspicious. Check and recheck the proposition. Ask advice from your accountant, bank manager and solicitor.

Buying a franchise

A franchise is the grant of a licence by one person (the franchiser) to another (the franchisee) which entitles the franchisee to trade under the franchiser's name. The franchisee will also receive help with establishing and running the business.

Before buying a franchise, there are some questions worth asking:

- Are the franchisers members of the British Franchise Association?
- Can they demonstrate success stories from other franchisees?
- Will they show you a sample contract, without commitment?
- Is the capital within your budget?
- Will the franchise be able to compete with other retailers in the high street, or with other service providers?
- How much time and money are you prepared to risk?

If buying a new franchise, publications which may contain useful information include *30 Ways to Make Money in Franchising* by Luke Johnson, the *Franchise Directory* (details on pp 125, 126) or the bi-monthly *Franchise World* magazine. It may also help to attend exhibitions, conferences and trade shows.

It is sometimes possible to buy an existing outlet if the franchiser is willing. The sale may be due to death or illness or the inability of the previous franchisee, in which case you might turn an existing failure into a future success. Treat the deal like the purchase of an ordinary business. Investigate its finances, turnover and profit margins. In the case of a retail business, study the site (rival businesses, numbers of passers-by, etc) and the conditions of the lease. If necessary, get the help of an accountant.

The franchises on offer in the United Kingdom include such household names as Alfred Marks, Clark's Shoes, Dyno Rod, Kentucky Fried Chicken, Prontoprint, Thorntons, Unigate Dairies and Wimpeys. There are also many smaller, recently established franchises. If you buy a franchise, you would expect to gain the following advantages:

- the right to use a recognised name and logo of which the public is already aware, so that your outlet will be regarded as an extension of a well-known enterprise;
- the exclusive right to the use of that name and logo within a given area for an agreed period;
- fewer start-up problems, since you will normally receive help with site selection, planning applications, design and furnishing of premises, choice of equipment, determination of stock levels, and profit forecasts and projections;
- initial training in the franchiser's methods; afterwards an operating manual provides guidance on such matters as accounting, marketing and stock control;
- the benefits derived from the franchiser's advertising, bulk-purchasing, and research and development.

One advantage for an older person is that the length of the agreement is negotiable. Agreements can be from five to fifteen years, with five years as an average. Most agreements contain an option to renew, subject to certain conditions.

Franchises do, however, have disadvantages. They can be costly: the initial fee charged can be from £5,000 to £400,000. In addition, you will need capital for premises, equipment, legal fees and stock. Afterwards royalties, based on turnover or profits, will be payable at agreed intervals to the franchiser.

They can also be restrictive. You will usually be obliged to buy goods and services from the franchiser, possibly at disadvantageous rates. Your scope for initiative and expansion will also be limited by the need to adhere to the franchiser's methods.

Difficulties can arise should you wish to dispose of the franchise. The franchiser will always require some say in approving a prospective purchaser; goodwill will remain the property of the franchiser even though it is you who have built it up.

As with the purchase of any other business, the contract between the franchiser and yourself should be submitted to your solicitor. Long before you have got to the contract stage, however, you should have carefully vetted the proposition yourself. A most useful checklist of 50 questions to put to the franchiser, prepared by Martin Mendelssohn, is available from the British Franchise Association (BFA) at the address on page 113. The BFA also provides an information pack which every prospective franchisee should obtain.

Offering a service

If you are about to retire but basically enjoy your job, you might like to carry on doing the same sort of work but on a freelance basis.

One good way of getting started as a freelance is by working for your former employer. Companies sometimes employ people in this way when they retire. Sometimes employers need to reduce their workforce but do not want to lose the valuable and sometimes irreplaceable services of skilled employees. In either case they might then subcontract work to a former employee, working on a freelance basis, as in the following examples:

Susan was employed by her firm as a full-time chiropodist. She was made redundant in a reorganisation of welfare services. The company still makes use of her services, however, by referring employees to her as an independent practitioner.

*   **Gilbert** worked at a pottery. One of his jobs was maintaining the linings of the kilns. When he retired his employers gave the work to an outside contractor, but the results were unsatisfactory. They therefore offered the work to Gilbert as a self-employed contractor. He now does work both for his old employer and for other firms in the area.*

It seems probable that organisations will in the future make increasing use of services provided by self-employed people. Offering some sort of service on a freelance basis could therefore be an ideal way of continuing to earn some money when you have retired. The service you offer might well make use of the skills you acquired while working, but you might choose instead to develop a hobby or leisure interest into a money-making activity, as in the following example:

*   **Joy,** an organist, wrote to a number of clergy informing them that she was available in the daytime on weekdays. She found that her services were in demand, particularly since she could play at funerals, weddings, etc when the regular church organist was often at work.*

Areas of activity particularly suitable for this approach include catering, computers, distribution, maintenance, office cleaning, printing, publicity, secretarial work and travel, but you could probably offer services in almost any area if you have the necessary skills and are able to market yourself effectively.

Of course, you may find not much marketing is needed. If, for example, you do your own dressmaking and are reasonably skilled, you may find enough people queuing up to have jobs done to keep you fully occupied.

Consultancy

Consultants are people who, because of their knowledge, skill or expertise, are approached by others for advice and assistance. Apart from those restricted by law to architects, medical practitioners and similar professions, there is virtually no limit to the areas in which you can set up as a consultant. You should, however, make sure that you comply with all regulations relating to a particular field of activity.

One of the main planks of the Financial Services Act, for example, is that Independent Financial Advisers (or consultants) must be authorised by a regulatory body such as the Financial Intermediaries, Managers and Brokers Regulatory Association (FIMBRA).

The term 'consultant' may be applied to fields as diverse as advertising, beauty, computers, fund-raising, tax and even retirement. Some businesses, eg solicitors, may keep on retired members as 'consultants'. They continue working for the firm in an advisory capacity and receive a retainer in return. Many retired executives become 'management consultants', as in the following example:

Rashid was chief buyer to a large engineering company. When one of his suppliers heard that he was retiring, they asked him to spend two or three days a week over a period of two months updating their purchasing and stores procedures. Rashid enjoyed the challenge. He installed a computerised stores system and also increased the contribution of the function to the profitability of the enterprise as a whole.

The experience revitalised Rashid's interest in purchasing and he attended two updating courses. On one of these, he met representatives of another company, who asked him to undertake a similar investigation for them. Rashid's former employer also asked him to write an updated procedure manual. These assignments convinced Rashid that his services were in demand. He had letterheads and business cards printed. Further work came through the local Chamber of Commerce. One year after he retired, he was working again – for himself.

Several aspects of the above case history are worth stressing:

- Rashid had expertise in a specific management field. Apart from 'General Management' you may, according to your qualifications and experience, become a consultant in virtually any aspect of business – advertising, finance, industrial relations, marketing, personnel, production, training and numerous others.

- His setting-up costs were small. Apart from the cost of the updating courses, his initial expenditure was restricted to that on letterheads and business cards.

- He kept up-to-date. You can only rely on experience for a limited time. Clients want up-to-date knowledge. Obtaining this can involve quite heavy expenditure on books, journals and research reports.
- Rashid exploited contacts, including his former suppliers and employer and people he met on the updating courses.
- He put the activity on a 'business footing'. As he became more established his expenditure expanded to include a computer with a word processing package, an answerphone and other office equipment. He also employed a part-time secretary. Very importantly, he convinced the Inland Revenue that he was self-employed (see pp 101–103).

Organisations tend to use consultants to obtain access to specialist skills which they do not possess themselves, and to obtain objectivity and independence of outlook in investigating problems and recommending how these should be solved. They are particularly likely to use consultants for short-term tasks, or where jobs or projects need to be completed in a short time.

Could you capitalise on your knowledge and experience by using them on a consultancy basis to earn in retirement? You are most likely to succeed if you agree before you start work what you are expected to do and what outcomes are to be achieved, and complete your assignment on time unless you are prevented by circumstances outside your control. Above all, do a good job. Successful consultancy businesses are built up by recommendations from satisfied clients.

What should you charge?

If you are self-employed, deciding how much to charge for your services is always extremely difficult. You will not want to price yourself out of the market, nor will you want to sell yourself ridiculously cheap.

Guidance on fees and charges is issued by some of the professional institutions such as the Law Society or the accountancy bodies. If you do not have professional status your fees will be substantially less. A bookkeeper may provide all the services of the professional accountant in respect of the accounts and tax matters of a small business at about a third of the cost. Individual management consultants will also be much cheaper than large consultancy firms.

There are several ways of fixing fees:

1 Charge 'what the traffic will bear', or what a prospective client is able and willing to pay.

2 Decide how much you wish to earn per week and how many hours you are prepared to work. If, for example, you wish to earn £100 per week, you will have to work 20 hours at £5 per hour, 10 hours at £10 or 5 hours at £20.

3 Do a costing exercise. Basically costs comprise three items: materials, labour and overheads.

If you are making a product you should have little difficulty in working out the cost of materials per item. You may be able to keep these to a minimum by buying in bulk.

If you are working for yourself, the labour cost will be what you consider a fair rate for the type of work you do. You can obtain an approximate idea of what is reasonable from the sources mentioned on page 81.

Overheads comprise expenses such as advertising, books or magazines for business use, depreciation of equipment, heating and lighting, postage, stationery, telephone bills, etc. You can calculate these accurately by totalling your estimated expenditure on these items for a year and dividing by the number of hours you expect to work. Thus, if all your expenses amount to £3,200 and you expect to work for 20 hours a week for 40 weeks, ie 800 hours a year, the overhead rate per hour will be 3,200 divided by 800, ie £4. If you add this to an hourly labour rate of £8, your fee per hour will be £12.

A rough and ready method is to add a fixed percentage for overheads, say 75 or 100 per cent, to your labour rate. If your labour rate is £8, a 75 per cent overhead of £6 will give you a total hourly rate of £14.

When deciding how much to charge, there are a few things you should remember:

- Do not under- or over-price yourself. In the latter case you will get little work. In the former case you will get insufficient pay for the work you do.
- Remember that time is the most precious commodity you have – do not undervalue it.
- Give value for money. Courtesy and a reputation for doing a good job will lead to a demand for your product or service.

Where can you go for help?

Local sources of help

Three of the most obvious sources of information and advice are your own bank manager, solicitor and accountant.

YOUR BANK MANAGER

You will need to see your bank manager when you open a separate business account. Bank managers are also an invaluable source of information on loans and other financial assistance. Your bank manager will be able to put you in touch with all the specialist services and information offered by all the major banks, including special packages for small business clients.

ACCOUNTANTS

It is not essential for you to employ an accountant, but unless you are an expert in bookkeeping and tax, you will normally find it advantageous to do so. Accountants' fees are usually charged on an hourly basis and can be costly, especially if you approach a member of either the Institute of Chartered Accountants or the Chartered Association of Certified Accountants.

In general, it is useful to distinguish between your daily bookkeeping requirements and the year-end preparation of final accounts which, when submitted to the Inland Revenue, will be the basis of your tax assessment. Bookkeeping is most economically undertaken on a part-time basis, possibly by someone else seeking to earn in retirement. The bookkeeper will make up your accounts weekly and possibly draft your year-end accounts for scrutiny by a professional accountant, who will deal with the Inland Revenue on your behalf.

It is also advisable to employ a professional accountant to examine the accounts of any existing business you contemplate buying as a going concern, particularly with regard to such items as goodwill, stocks, turnover and profits.

Accountants will provide you with details of their charges and services offered. Failure to employ a professional accountant may be a case of 'penny-wise, pound-foolish'. In any case, remember that accountancy fees are tax-deductible expenses.

SOLICITORS

Solicitors will be essential when you require legal advice or services relating to contracts, employment matters, consumer protection and the purchase or sale of property. Lawyers for Enterprise have a business advice scheme offering a free initial consultation with a solicitor to anyone contemplating setting up in business (phone 071–405 9075 for details).

CHAMBERS OF COMMERCE

Chambers of Commerce also offer a wide range of advice and assistance to anyone wishing to establish a business. Look in your *Yellow Pages* under 'Chambers of Commerce' for the local address.

LOCAL ENTERPRISE AGENCIES

Another source of help are Local Enterprise Agencies. These are partnerships of local businesses, Chambers of Commerce, local authorities and professions that aim to stimulate the starting and expansion of small businesses by offering business advice and counselling (usually free) and often additional services such as access to loan funds, managed work space, business clubs and information services. There are about 400 such agencies in England and Wales. Enterprise Trusts are the Scottish equivalent. Details of the nearest Local Enterprise Agency can be obtained by dialling 0800 444246.

Government assistance

The Government also offers various forms of assistance to anyone wishing to set up their own business. From 1991 schemes formerly administered by the Training Agency will become the responsibility of 82 Training and Enterprise Councils or TECs. For the address of your nearest TEC, dial 0800 444246.

What is mainly on offer is advice and training. The Business Enterprise Programme, for example, offers short courses and an open learning package on basic business training to anyone contemplating starting their own business. The Small Firms Service, sponsored by the Department of Trade and Industry, provides a free telephone enquiry service and in-depth business counselling for the London area. A useful range of pamphlets and a free book, *Starting and Running Your Own Business,* are also available. The Small Firms Service also provides opportunities for experienced business men and women, including those who have recently retired, to serve as counsellors, for which a daily payment is made. Phone them on 0800 222999.

Business Growth Training does, however, offer some financial help to small businesses as well as a range of free kits, low-cost seminars and other specialist advice, while the Enterprise Allowance Scheme offers £40 a week to anyone wishing to set up their own business. You must be between 18 and 65, unemployed, have a good business plan, and be able to invest £1,000 in the business over the first 12 months. How long you need to have been unemployed varies according to area – contact your local TEC to see if you qualify.

Educational institutions

If you are interested in training, it is worth remembering that colleges, polytechnics and universities are increasingly able to meet the professional, industrial and commercial (PICKUP) training needs of small and medium-sized firms, and also provide advice and consultancy services. For details phone the Department of Education and Science on 071-934 9000 (address on p 114).

If you feel you are unlikely to be able to attend a course regularly, open learning courses enable people to study at their own pace when business pressures permit (see pp 46–47 for more about open learning). A wide variety of short and long courses is now available. For details consult the *Directory of Open Learning Opportunities*, which may be available in your local reference library. For other organisations that might be worth contacting for advice and support if you are thinking of starting a business, see pages 118–120.

Your tax position

Obtaining self-employed status

For taxation purposes it is important to determine whether your earnings derive from employment or self-employment. If the Inland Revenue regard you as self-employed, expenditure you incur in the course of earning your income may be allowed against tax, which can save a substantial amount of money.

People classed as employees may claim for only a very few items of expenditure. If you are self-employed you may, for example, claim for the costs of travelling from home to your place of work and back, but if you are an employee you may claim only for travelling expenses actually incurred in performing your duties. You cannot claim for the costs of travelling to and from home.

If you are self-employed you may be able to claim for:
- Accountancy fees
- Advertising expenditure
- Bad debts
- Clerical assistance

- Cost of materials used
- Expenditure on answerphone, telephone, postage, stationery, relevant periodicals
- A proportion of your motoring expenses
- Repairs and maintenance of typewriter or word processor
- Travelling and hotel expenses incurred for business purposes
- Use of your home where your home is your place of business

This last can comprise a proportion of the total costs of cleaning, heating, insurance, lighting, maintenance, rent and rates. Make sure that no one room is exclusively used for business purposes, otherwise you may partially forfeit the Capital Gains Tax exemption on the house as your only or main residence. The usual procedure is to claim a deduction on the basis that most or all of the rooms are used for business purposes.

You may also claim for work done by your spouse, eg bookkeeping, cleaning, reception or typing, providing that the amounts claimed, which should be at the market rate, are actually paid. You cannot, however, claim for the cost of business entertaining or improvements to premises.

For more details about what you can and cannot claim, contact your accountant or your local tax office.

WHO DECIDES IF YOU ARE SELF-EMPLOYED?

The fact that you regard yourself as self-employed will not automatically mean the Inland Revenue will accord you self-employed status.

If you set up a business and wish to claim you are self-employed, seek an interview with your local tax inspector, who will decide on your claim. The tax inspector will apply a number of criteria, including:

- Do your earnings derive from one or several sources? If from only one source, you will have greater difficulty in persuading the tax inspector to regard you as self-employed.

- How much control is exercised over what you do and when you do it? If you work regular hours, are entitled to stated holidays, or receive specific instructions on how to do the work, you are likely to be regarded as an employee.

If you are dissatisfied with the tax inspector's decision as to whether you are self-employed, you can appeal. Your tax inspector will explain the procedure.

Remember, however, that it is possible to be taxed both as an employee and as self-employed. Thus you could be employed during the day and work in the evenings as, say, a freelance writer.

Personal pension plans

There is a distinction between legal tax avoidance and illegal tax evasion through not declaring your earnings. While there are heavy penalties for tax evasion, it is only good sense to use the many allowances, exemptions and reliefs contained in tax legislation to the best advantage. One of the best ways to reduce tax on your retirement earnings or profits is to take out a personal pension plan, as you are allowed full tax relief on the contributions you make to it.

The amount you are allowed to contribute to your personal pension plan is not, however, unlimited. The maximum contribution you can make is worked out as a percentage of your net pensionable earnings (ie earnings from a trade, profession or non-pensionable employment, for a given year, after deduction of allowable expenses). The percentage is based on your age at the start of the income tax year, the amount you are allowed to contribute increasing as you get older.

There is also a limit on net pensionable earnings. This means that even if your net pensionable earnings are more than the limit, the most you can contribute is the appropriate percentage of the limit. The limit is increased annually in line with inflation.

The advantages of using part of your earnings in this way can be seen from an example:

John took early retirement at the age of 55. He set up as a management consultant on 1 April. His net relevant earnings (NRE) for the year averaged £910 monthly. As he had other income from a pension and investments, he decided to pay 25 per cent of his NRE into a personal pension plan, ie £227.50 a month.

Assuming John pays tax at 25 per cent, the actual cost of his gross monthly contribution would be £227.50, but he would only have to pay £170.62 because he would save £56.88 in income tax, ie 25 per cent of the contribution.

If monthly contributions were maintained at this level for five years until John finally retired at the age of 60, and with interest rates between 8.5 and 13 per cent, he would receive a cash sum of £4,450–£5,020 and a monthly pension of between £128 and £163 for the rest of his life.

When negotiating a personal pension plan there are two maxims that at first sight seem contradictory. First, do not be precipitate. Make sure you get the best plan for you. Look in the *Handbook for Self-Employed Pensions,* available in a good reference library. This will give much useful information and provide the names of companies that specialise in this business. Look through back copies of *Money Management* magazine, which publishes periodical performance tables. Approach several selected companies and compare what they offer.

Banks, building societies and financial advisers will all give you information and advice, but almost invariably they will recommend their own products. If you go to a broker, they must tell you whether they are 'tied', that is an agent of one company and able to recommend only that company's products. Advice on a whole range of financial products can be given by 'independent' brokers, but as they mostly earn their money on a commission basis, the advice is not necessarily the best. Fees may be charged instead of commission. *Money Management* magazine has a list of advisers who charge fees and will supply to members of the public, free of charge, six names in the relevant postal area (phone 071–405 6969).

Second, do not hesitate too long. The longer the delay, the lower will be the benefits. The amount of pension lost as a result of delaying a plan for one year can be substantial.

CHAPTER SIX

Working for a voluntary agency

What about doing some voluntary work?

What exactly is a voluntary agency?

How do I set about finding voluntary work?

Could I get a paid job with a voluntary agency?

As mentioned in Chapter 1, earning money is by no means the only motive for working in retirement. Especially if you are retiring early, you may be keen to make constructive use of your time, and retain a sense of purposefulness and a feeling that you are still part of the community. You may value the opportunity to do something completely different from your pre-retirement job and perhaps even to acquire new skills. You may also miss the work environment and the companionship of the people you worked with. If your motives for wanting to work after you have retired are of this sort, and you do not particularly need extra money, you may well find that doing some voluntary work is just as satisfying as doing a paid job – or even more so.

The opportunities for doing voluntary work are almost limitless. You could do work for your church, or for a political, sporting or other organisation, or you could run errands for your elderly neighbours, but you are most likely to find suitable work with a voluntary agency, of which there are vast numbers, engaged in many different fields of activity.

What is a voluntary agency?

Voluntary agencies must be non-profit-distributing (ie all profits are ploughed back into the organisation) and of public benefit. Although many receive funds from the State, they are constitutionally separate from the Government. They range from national charities such as Oxfam and Age Concern and campaigning bodies such as Friends of the Earth to community groups and local action groups.

The following classification of the work carried out by voluntary agencies, produced by the National Council for Voluntary Organisations (NCVO), gives some idea of the scope of the work they do.

Work with children and young people
Helping in playgroups, youth clubs, scouts, guides, Boys' Brigade.

Work with elderly people

Helping with shopping or gardening, or with meals on wheels, helping at day centres or old people's homes.

Work in hospitals

Visiting patients, providing transport to and from appointments, after-care visiting, organising book and magazine loans. Some hospitals have their own voluntary services co-ordinator and/or League of Friends.

Advice work

Work in a Citizens Advice Bureau or law centre, for which training will normally have to be undertaken.

Counselling

Covers relationship problems, alcohol, drug and gambling problems, victim support, youth counselling, the Samaritans. The British Association for Counselling (address on p 121) publishes a *Counselling and Psychotherapy Resources Directory.*

Conservation and the environment

Restoring canals, uncovering archaeological sites, working on organic farms or city farms. The British Trust for Conservation Volunteers (address on p 113) is the main source of information regarding possibilities in this field.

People with special needs

Reading to blind people, providing practical support for someone with a physical disability, helping in an adult literacy scheme. There are numerous possibilities for working with voluntary agencies serving people with a specific disability or disease such as the Royal Society for Mentally Handicapped Children and Adults or the Multiple Sclerosis Society. Such organisations are listed in the *Voluntary Agencies Directory, Health Directory* or *Parents' Directory* (details on pp 125, 126), which should be available in your local reference library.

Campaigning

Becoming active in a campaigning organisation, whether a national one such as Friends of the Earth or one that campaigns on local issues, such as lobbying against a planning application you feel is detrimental to your local area.

Miscellaneous

Getting involved in a project to help homeless people; work with ex-offenders or prisoners; setting up a self-help group for a particular illness or category of people; work with animals.

In addition, all voluntary agencies need people to help with fund-raising – organising fund-raising events like jumble sales or sponsored walks, working in a charity shop, helping with a flag day, putting together applications for grants from trusts, companies or government bodies. And a great many local groups are always on the lookout for people willing to serve on their management committees.

What can you offer?

In general, as a retired person, you will be able to offer time, experience and expertise.

Time

You can decide which time of the day and week you want to volunteer. The organisation you are helping can then decide how best to use the time placed at its disposal. But if some other time would be particularly helpful to the organisation, you may well feel able to comply: ready availability – indeed time itself – is one of the great assets of retired people.

Experience

Experience does not simply mean your experience at work. Retired people are often more acceptable as counsellors and helpers to those in their own age group because they have lived through the same period of history and weathered the same difficulties. Such experience is particularly relevant when volunteers work with individual clients, often in sensitive and demanding roles, as in the following example:

Donald, a former university lecturer, because of his age and background was asked to help John , aged 57, who had been found guilty of shoplifting. John, Principal of a College of Further Education, had resigned his post because of the publicity given to the case and become withdrawn and depressed. It was hoped that he might benefit from the friendship of someone who shared his intellectual interests and had also served in the Second World War. Donald and John quickly became friends. Over a period of nine months Donald helped John to regain his self-esteem and rebuild his social life.

Expertise

As a retired person you can make available voluntarily the skills and expertise acquired in your working life. A former accountant might become treasurer of a local group, while a former manager or manageress of a shop might help run a charity shop.

But the expertise may not be related to your pre-retirement job. An Age Concern report on how retired people spent their time gave examples of, among others, a former worker on British Rail who trained boys at a boxing club and a former secretary who visited hospitals and homes, teaching handicrafts. In addition, some voluntary agencies, such as the Citizens Advice Bureaux, the Samaritans and Relate (formerly Marriage Guidance), do offer training. Given that you are willing to work unpaid, it is worthwhile for them to provide you with training – something employers are unfortunately much less likely to offer to older people who are being paid for their work. This training could obviously be useful if you decide to return to paid work at a later date.

How to find voluntary work

If you have already been taking part in some voluntary activity, retirement may simply provide an opportunity for greater participation in that activity, as in the following example:

Maureen has been providing secretarial work one evening a week to her local Women's Royal Voluntary Service office. On retirement she intends to undertake additional WRVS training and offer her services in the daytime and at weekends as well.

If you are not already involved in a voluntary activity, you will have to do a bit more research – although you may well hear of voluntary agencies that are looking for helpers through your own 'networks' (see pp 65–66), and even become interested in a branch of voluntary activity you had not previously considered.

The most important sources of voluntary work are the local and national voluntary agencies themselves, and specialised employment agencies.

A list of local voluntary agencies should be obtainable from your local reference library, Citizens Advice Bureau or Council of Social Service. There are probably more voluntary agencies in your locality than you imagine. On a national level, the NCVO, and its equivalents in Northern Ireland, Scotland and Wales, and the Volunteer Centre both publish useful information leaflets relating to employment opportunities, both paid and unpaid, in the voluntary sector.

Some directories have already been mentioned in this chapter. Perhaps the most comprehensive general one is the *Voluntary Agencies Directory*, found in most reference libraries, which lists nearly 2,000 national voluntary agencies. It is also useful to look at the voluntary agencies listed under the headings of 'charitable and benevolent organisations' and 'social service and welfare organisations' in your local *Yellow Pages*.

REACH, the Retired Executives Action Clearing House, specialises in funding part-time 'expenses only' jobs for retired business men and women who want to use their skills to help voluntary agencies with charitable aims throughout Great Britain. Although most REACH placements – there are about 500 annually – are local and low-profile, there are exceptions. One former Unilever executive was placed with the Centre for International Peacebuilding. Within a year he had attended a conference in Moscow and spent an afternoon in the company of Mikhail Gorbachev in the Kremlin.

Opportunities for paid work with voluntary agencies

While in a minority of cases it may be true that doing voluntary work implies that your help is acceptable providing it does not have to be paid for, most organisations would be happy to pay if they could. Because they cannot do so they have to rely on the dedication of helpers who believe what they are doing is worthwhile for its own sake. But, as we have already seen (p 109), some voluntary agencies do offer useful training, and some offer opportunities to travel with expenses paid. If you are found a job by REACH, your expenses will be paid. Occasionally, very large companies second their senior employees to work in a voluntary agency for a few months before they retire.

There are also opportunities for paid work with voluntary agencies in a variety of posts. Since the pay offered for such posts is based on what the organisation can afford, which is often substantially less than comparable rates obtainable in commerce, industry and the public service, a retired person who can use the remuneration received to supplement their pension is often attractive to voluntary sector employers. If you have experience of working for a voluntary agency as a volunteer, that will certainly stand you in good stead if you do decide to apply for a paid job.

Paid posts are often advertised in the local and national press. The *Guardian* Public Appointments issue published on Wednesdays is especially useful. A list of other publications in which vacancies may be advertised is given in NCVO Information Sheet 21, *Employment Opportunities in the Voluntary Sector – Paid Employment*.

Three agencies specialise in recruiting staff for charities, namely, the Charity Recruitment Executive Register, Charity Appointments and the Raine Partnership. And there is of course nothing to stop you selecting a number of voluntary agencies from one of the directories mentioned earlier and sending a copy of your cv to them.

One further possibility open to people with the requisite skills and experience who have retired early in good health is work abroad. You are most likely to obtain such work if you possess appropriate qualifications and experience in the fields of administration, agriculture, civil engineering, education or health. Five organisations that can provide further information are the British Council, the Catholic Institute for International Relations, IVS Overseas, the United Nations Association and Voluntary Service Overseas (addresses on pp 113–116).

If you are thinking of working as a volunteer for a voluntary agency, remember that you are more likely to work well if the cause is one in which you strongly believe. Only volunteer for what you are sure you will be able to do well, and only undertake voluntary work if you are certain you will be able to give reliable help over a reasonable period of time. It is not easy to do a job consistently and conscientiously for no pay, so it is best not to be over-ambitious but only to offer what you are sure you will be able to stick to.

When working as a volunteer, it is easy to slip into offering to do more and more. As with any form of paid work, the more time you give to voluntary work the less time you will have for your family and other activities. As always, it is important to keep the balance right.

All these cautions apart, working for a voluntary agency in retirement can give you much in return. Above all, it can give you the chance to show your concern for others, and actually do something about social problems.

Further information

Useful addresses

Advisory Board of Ministry
Church House
Great Smith Street
London SW1P 3NZ
Tel: 071-222 9011

Association of Retired Persons
Membership Centre
Broughwoods House
Shillingford
Bampton
Devon EX16 9BL
Tel: 0398 6485

British Council
10 Spring Gardens
London SW1A 2BN
Tel: 071-930 8466

British Franchise Association
Franchise Chambers
Thames View
Newtown Road
Henley on Thames
Oxon RG9 1HG
Tel: 0491 578049

British Trust for Conservation Volunteers
36 St Mary's Street
Wallingford
Oxon OX10 OEU
Tel: 0491 39766

Catholic Institute for International Relations Overseas Programme
Unit 3
Cannonbury Yard
190A New North Road
London N1 7BJ
Tel: 071–354 0883

Centre for Policy on Ageing
25–31 Ironmonger Row
London EC1V 3QP
Tel: 071–253 1787

Charity Appointments
3 Spital Yard
Bishopsgate
London E1 6AQ
Tel: 071–247 4502

Charity Recruitment
Executive Register
40 Rosebery Avenue
London EC1R 4RN
Tel: 071–833 0770

**City and Guilds of
London Institute**
46 Britannia Street
London WC1X 9RG
Tel: 071–278 2468

**Department of Education
and Science**
Elizabeth House
39 York Road
London SE1 7PH
Tel: 071–934 9000

**Department of Employment
Wages Inspectorate**
2nd Floor, Alexandra House
14–22 Parsonage Gardens
Manchester M3 2JS
Tel: 061–832 6506

Homesitters Ltd
Buckland Wharf
Buckland
Aylesbury
Bucks HP22 5LQ
Tel: 0296 630730

**House of Studies for
Late Vocations**
Campion House College
112 Thornbury Road
Isleworth
Middlesex TW7 4NN
Tel: 081–560 1924

IVS Overseas
188 Round Hay Road
Leeds LS8 5PL
Tel: 0532 406787

**National Council for
Voluntary Organisations**
26 Bedford Square
London WC1B 2HU
Tel: 071–636 4066

**Northern Ireland Council
for Voluntary Action**
127 Ormeau Road
Belfast BT7 1SH.
Tel: 0232 321 224

**Occupational Pensions
Advisory Service**
11 Belgrave Road
London SW1V 1RB
Tel: 071–233 8080

The Open College
Saint Paul's
781 Wilmslow Road
Didsbury
Greater Manchester M20 8RW
Tel: 061–434 0007

**Open University Central
Enquiries Office**
PO Box 200
Walton Hall
Milton Keynes MK7 6YZ
Tel: 0908 653231

**Pre-Retirement Association
of Great Britain
and Northern Ireland**
Nodus Centre
University Campus
Guildford GU2 5RX
Tel: 0483 39323

**Pre-School Playgroups
Association**
61–63 Kings Cross Road
London WC1X 9LL
Tel: 071–833 0991

Raine
13 Prince of Wales Terrace
London W8 5PG
Tel: 071–937 4454

**Registrar of Pension Schemes
Occupational Pensions Board**
PO Box 1NN
Newcastle upon Tyne
NE99 1NN
Tel: 091–225 6389

Retirement Trust
39 St James's Street
London SW1A 1JQ
Tel: 071–408 4936

**Scottish Council for
Voluntary Organisations**
18–19 Claremont Crescent
Edinburgh EH7 4QD
Tel: 031–556 3882

**Scottish Institute of Adult
and Continuing Education**
30 Rutland Square
Edinburgh EH1 2BW
Tel: 031–229 0331

Scottish Retirement Council
Alexandra House
204 Bath Street
Glasgow G2 4HL
Tel: 041–332 9427

**Training, Enterprise and
Education Directorate (TEED)**
Moorfoot
Sheffield S1 4PQ
Tel: 0742 753275

**United Nations Association
International Service**
Suite 3A, Hunter House
57 Goodrangate
York YO1 2LS
Tel: 0904 647 799

Universal Aunts
PO Box 304
London SW4 0NN
Tel: 071–738 8937

Voluntary Service Overseas (VSO)
317 Putney Bridge Road
London SW15 2PN
Tel: 081–780 2266

Volunteer Centre
29 Lower Kings Road
Berkhampsted
Herts HP4 2AB
Tel: 0442 873311

Wales Council for Voluntary Action
Llys Ifor
Crescent Road
Cearffili CF8 1XL
Tel: 0222 869 224/5/6

Workers' Educational Association
Temple House
9 Upper Berkeley Street
London W1H 8BY
Tel: 071–402 5608

Employment agencies for older people

Age Works
ECCO Employment Agency
3rd Floor, Bedford House
69–79 Fulham High Street
London SW6 3JW
Tel: 071–371 5411

Buretire (Bureau for the Retired)
Head Office
Willowthorpe
High Street
Stanstead Abbotts
Herts SG12 8AS
Tel: 0920 870158

Offices in Bishops Stortford, Cambridge, Letchworth, Waltham Cross and Walthamstow

Corps of Commissionaires
Head Office
Market House
85 Cowcross Street
London EC1M 6BP
Tel: 071–490 1125

Executive Standby
310 Chester Road
Hartford
Northwich
Cheshire CW8 2AB
Tel: 0606 883849

Executive Standby (South)
51 London Wool and Fruit Exchange
Brushfield Street
London E1 6EU
Tel: 071–247 5693

Executive Standby (West)
Somercourt
Holmfield Road
Saltford
Bristol BS18 3EG
Tel: 0225 873118

Officers' Association
48 Pall Mall
London SW1Y 5JY
Tel: 071–930 0125

Part-Time Careers Ltd
10 Golden Square
London W1R 3AF
Tel: 071–437 3103

Reach (Retired Executives Action Clearing House)
89 Southwark Street
London SE1 OHD
Tel: 071–928 0452

Regular Forces Employment Association
Head Office
25 Bloomsbury Square
London WC1A 2LN
Tel: 071–637 3918

Royal British Legion Attendants Co Ltd
Head Office
2A Rathmore Road
London SE7 7QW
Tel: 081–305 1218

Regional offices in Cambridge, Cardiff, Leeds, London, Preston and Poole

Success After Sixty
40–41 Old Bond Street
London W1X 3AF
Tel: 071–629 0672

Organisations offering help to self-employed people and small businesses

British Coal Enterprise Ltd
Provides help to businesses contemplating setting up or expanding in a traditional coal-mining area, including low-interest loans, help in finding premises, and retraining for redundant British Coal employees.

60 Station Road
Sutton in Ashfield
Nottingham
NG17 5GA
Tel: 0623 442244

British Steel Industry Ltd
Performs a similar service to the above in traditional steel areas.

Bridge House
Bridge Street
Sheffield S3 8NS
Tel: 0742 731612

Federation of Small Businesses
Promotes and protects the interests of small businesses. Members receive a bi-monthly magazine, First Voice, *24–hour free legal advice, and help with court costs.*

140 Lower Marsh
Westminster Bridge
London SE1 7AE
Tel: 071–928 9272

IMMPACT
IMMPACTis a self-help organisation for older workers. Members aim to combine their skills and experience to begin their own businesses and offer support during periods of unemployment.

National Office
5 South Street
Reading
Berkshire RG1 4QP

Institute of Management Consultants
For management consultancy firms rather than individuals. Their Directory of Member Firms *may help you to locate consultancies to whom your services could be offered. The Institute also publishes a number of useful booklets.*

5th Floor
32–33 Hatton Gardens
London EC1N 8DL
Tel: 071–242 2140

Lawyers for Enterprise
Offers free initial consultation with a
solicitor to anyone starting up a
business.

50–52 Chancery Lane
London WC2A 1SX
Tel: 071–242 1222

National Extension College
Offers several training packs, including
Be Your Own Boss, Starting and
Growth Kits and You and Your
Business.

18 Brooklands Avenue
Cambridge CB2 2HN
Tel: 0223 316644

Rural Development Commission
Provides businesses in rural areas with
free general advice, in-depth technical
and professional support, help in
converting and acquiring premises, and
gives limited loans and grants.

141 Castle Street
Salisbury
Wiltshire SP1 3TP
Tel: 0722 336255

Women's Enterprise Development
Agency (WEDA)
Aims to promote women's self-
employment in non-traditional areas.
Provides training, practical advice, help
and on-going support to would-be
business women.

Aston Science Park
Love Lane
Aston Triangle
Birmingham B7 4BJ
Tel: 021–359 0178

Women in Enterprise
Aims to encourage women
entrepreneurs to set up their own
businesses. It provides practical
information at regional level. Please
write, enclosing sae.

4 Co-operative Street
Horbury
Wakefield WF4 6DR

Selected organisations for specific occupations or hobbies

BOOKKEEPING

Association of Accounting Technicians
The professional body for skilled support staff working in accounting and finance. People who are not professionally qualified can take the Association exams.

154 Clerkenwell Road
London EC1R 5AD
Tel: 071–837 8600

CARERS

Carers' National Association
Provides information and support to carers. It also puts carers in touch with each other through its network of local groups and branches.

29 Chilworth Mews
London W2 3RG
Tel: 071–724 7776

CHILDMINDING

National Childminding Association
Set up in 1977 to enhance the profile of childminders and all aspects of childminding. Gives advice and support to childminders and parents.

8 Masons Hill
Bromley
Kent BR2 9EY
Tel: 081–464 6164

CLOCK AND WATCH REPAIRING

British Horological Institute
Offers a correspondence course in technical horology. Enthusiasts may enrol as associate members without taking any examination.

Upton Hall
Upton
Newark
Notts NG23 5TE
Tel: 0636 813795

COMPUTING

Association of Computer Professionals
Holds examinations in computing and provides other services for people wishing to work in the computing field.

204 Barnett Wood Lane
Ashstead
Surrey KT21 2DB
Tel: 0372 273442

Association of Business and Administrative Computing
As the above.

Shaftesbury Centre
Percy Street
Swindon
Wiltshire SN5 9LD
Tel: 0793 514055

British Computer Society
As the above.

PO Box 1454
Station Road
Swindon SN1 1TG
Tel: 0793 480269

COUNSELLING

British Association for Counselling
Membership open to anyone working as a counsellor, using counselling skills in their work, or training to be a counsellor. Can provide details of career training opportunities.

1 Regent Place
Rugby
Warwickshire
CV21 2PJ
Tel: 0788 578328

CRAFTS

Crafts Council
Covers a wide range of craft activities.

44A Pentonville Road
London N1 9BY
Tel: 071-178 7700

DIRECT SELLING

Direct Selling Association
All DSA member companies abide by a strict code of practice. If considering any form of direct selling, you are advised to ensure that the organisation you join is a DSA member.

29 Floral Street
London WC2E 9DP
Tel: 071–497 1234

HOME-MADE PRODUCE

National Federation of Women's Institutes
Markets usually held one morning a week. New producers, who need not be WI members, should contact the Controller of the nearest WI market for details.

Markets Department
104 New Kings Road
Fulham
London SW6 4LY
Tel: 071–371 9300

HOMEWORKING AS ASSEMBLERS, PACKERS, ETC

Greater Manchester Low-Pay Unit
Publishes a Homeworkers Information Pack for homeworkers in the Manchester area. Similar packs are produced by other local organisations.

23 New Mount Street
Manchester M4 4DE
Tel: 061–953 4024

Low Pay Unit
Advises on pay and employment rights.

9 Upper Berkeley Street
London W1H 8BY
Tel: 071–262 7278

INDEXING

Society of Indexers
Maintains a register of members of proven practical competence. Provides introductions to authors, publishers and others who commission indexes.

16 Green Road
Birchington
Kent CT7 9JZ
Tel: 0843 41115

LANGUAGES AND TRANSLATION

Institute of Linguists
The Institute's examinations provide a benchmark of practical language skills, providing valuable qualificational levels from basic to advanced.

24A Highbury Grove
London N5 2EA
Tel: 071–359 7445

Translators' Association
An organisation for literary translators. Members must have at least one work translated in the UK.

Society of Authors
84 Drayton Gardens
London SW10 9SD
Tel: 071–373 6642

TEACHING

Association of British Correspondence Colleges
Will provide a list of accredited correspondence colleges, who may be looking for qualified persons interested in teaching by distance learning.

6 Francis Grove
London SW19 4DT

Council for the Accreditation of Correspondence Colleges
Will supply similar information to the above.

27 Marylebone Road
London NW1 5JS
Tel: 071–935 5391

Incorporated Society of Musicians
Open to private music teachers, generally with professional music qualifications. Provides a register of private music teachers and makes recommendations regarding fees.

10 Stratford Place
London W1N 9AE
Tel: 071–629 4413

National Union of Journalists
A trade union for working journalists. Publishes a Freelance Directory *and a* Freelance Fees Guide *in addition to* Journalist, *the union's official organ.*

Acorn House
314 Gray's Inn Road
London WC1X 8DP
Tel: 071-278 7916

Society of Authors
Provides many services to members, including information about agents, publishers and others concerned with the book trade, journalism, broadcasting and the performing arts.

84 Drayton Gardens
London SW10 9SD
Tel: 071–373 6642

Writers Guild of Great Britain
The writers' trade union. Gives advice to individual members on any aspect of their business life, including contracts, agents, publishers and fees.

430 Edgware Road
London W2 1EH
Tel: 071–723 8074

Useful publications

The A–Z of Self-Employment, Bloch, Sidney (Buchan and Enright).

The Best is Yet to Come: A Workbook for the Middle Years, Smith, Maggie (Lifeskills Associates).

Branching Out: A Workbook for Early Retirement, Smith, Maggie (Lifeskills Associates).

British Qualifications (Kogan Page).

Careers in Crafts, Garnier (Kogan Page).

Counselling and Psychotherapy Resources Directory (British Association for Counselling).

The Daily Mail Guide to Working from Home (Harmsworth Publications).

Directory of Open Learning Opportunities (Training Agency).

Directory of Pre-Retirement Courses. Available from Nodus Centre, University Campus, Guildford, Surrey GU2 5RX.

Earning Money at Home (Consumers' Association).

Franchise Directory (Franchise Development Services).

Franchising: A Small Business Guide, Fowler, Alan and Fowler, Deborah (Sphere).

Getting Started: How to Set Up Your Own Business, Robson, Rhodes (Kogan Page).

Going Freelance: Self-Employment with Minimum Capital, Golzen, Godfrey (Kogan Page).

The Good Retirement Guide, Brown, Rosemary (Kogan Page).

The Guardian Guide to Running a Small Business, ed Woodcock, Clive (Kogan Page).

Health Directory, compiled by MacDonald, Fiona (Bedford Square Press).

How to Start a Business from Home, Jones, Graham (Northcote House Publishers).

How to Start, Run and Stay in Business, Kishel, Gregory F and Kishel, Patricia Gunter (Wiley).

The New Unemployment Handbook, Dauncey, Guy (National Extension College).

Parents' Directory, ed MacDonald, Fiona (Bedford Square Press).

Part-Time Work, Humphries, Judith (Kogan Page).

Second Chances: A National Guide to Adult Education and Training Opportunities, Good, Martin and Pates, Andrew. Available from Careers and Occupational Information Centre, The Paddock, Frizinghall, Bradford BD9 4HD.

Starting a Small Business, Fowler, Alan and Fowler, Deborah (Sphere).

Starting and Running Your Own Business (Small Firms Service). Available from Small Firms Service, 11 Belgrave Road, London SW13 1RB.

Starting Your Own Business (Consumers' Association).

Student Grants and Loans (Department of Education and Science). Available from local education authorities.

Training and Retraining to Teach Priority Subjects. Available from Department of Education and Science, Elizabeth House, 39 York Road, London SE1 7PH.

Voluntary Agencies Directory (Bedford Square Press).

Working for Yourself: Daily Telegraph Guide to Self-Employment, Golzen, Godfrey (Kogan Page).

Working from Home: 201 Ways to Earn Money, Gray, Marianne (Piatkus).

30 Ways to Make Money in Franchising, Johnson, Luke (Rosters)

About Age Concern

Earning Money in Retirement is one of a wide range of publications produced by Age Concern England – National Council on Ageing. In addition, Age Concern is actively engaged in training, information provision, research and campaigning for retired people and those who work with them. It is a registered charity dependent on public support for the continuation of its work.

Age Concern England links closely with Age Concern centres in Scotland, Wales and Northern Ireland to form a network of over 1,400 independent local UK groups. These groups, with the invaluable help of an estimated 250,000 volunteers, aim to improve the quality of life for older people and develop services appropriate to local needs and resources. These include advice and information, day care, visiting services, transport schemes, clubs, and specialist facilities for physically and mentally frail older people.

Age Concern England
1268 London Road
London SW16 4ER
Tel: 081–679 8000

Age Concern Scotland
54a Fountainbridge
Edinburgh EH3 9PT
Tel: 031–228 5656

Age Concern Wales
4th Floor
1 Cathedral Road
Cardiff CF1 9SD
Tel: 0222 371566

Age Concern Northern Ireland
6 Lower Crescent
Belfast BT7 1NR
Tel: 0232 245729

Publications from ◆C◐ Books

A wide range of titles is published by Age Concern England under the ACE Books imprint.

HEALTH AND CARE

In Control: Help with incontinence

Penny Mares

Containing information about the nature and causes of incontinence and the sources of help available, this book has been written for anyone concerned about this problem, either professionally or at home. The text is illustrated with diagrams and case histories.

£4.50   0-86242-088-1

Your Health in Retirement

Dr J A Muir Gray and Pat Blair

This book is a comprehensive source of information to help readers look after themselves and work towards better health. Produced in an easy-to-read A–Z style, full details are given of people and useful organisations from which advice and assistance can be sought.

£4.50   0–86242–082–2

The Magic of Movement

Laura Mitchell

Full of encouragement, this book is for those who are finding everyday activities more difficult. Includes gentle exercises to tone up muscles and ideas to make you more independent and avoid boredom.

£3.95   0–86242–076–8

Know Your Medicines

Pat Blair

We would all like to know more about the medicines we take. The second edition of this successful guide, for older people and their carers, examines how the body works and the effects of medication.

£6.95   0-86242-100-4

MONEY MATTERS

Your Rights
Sally West

A highly acclaimed annual guide to the State Benefits available to older people. Contains current information on Income Support, Housing Benefit and retirement pensions, among other matters, and provides advice on how to claim them.

Further information on application

Your Taxes and Savings
Jennie Hawthorne and Sally West

Explains how the tax system affects people over retirement age, including how to avoid paying more tax than is necessary. The information about savings covers the wide range of investment opportunities now available.

Further information on application

Using Your Home as Capital
Cecil Hinton

This best-selling book for home owners, which is updated annually, gives a detailed explanation of how to capitalise on the value of your home and obtain a regular additional income.

Further information on application

Managing Other People's Money
Penny Letts

The management of money and property is usually a personal and private matter. However, there may come a time when someone else has to take over on either a temporary or a permanent basis. This book looks at the circumstances in which such a need could arise and provides a step-by-step guide to the arrangements which have to be made.

£5.95   0–86242–090–3

GENERAL

Living, Loving and Ageing: Sexual and personal relationships in later life
Wendy Greengross and Sally Greengross
Sexuality is often regarded as the preserve of the younger generation. This book, for older people and those who work with them, tackles the issues in a straightforward fashion, avoiding preconceptions and bias.
£4.95   0–86242–070–9

Looking Good, Feeling Good: Fashion and beauty in mid-life and beyond
Nancy Tuft
Positive, upbeat and awash with useful advice and ideas, this book encourages the over 50s to take pride in their appearance and challenges the popular view that interest in fashion and beauty passes with the years. Illustrated in full colour.
£7.95   0–86242–102–0

Gardening in Retirement
Isobel Pays
Introduction by Percy Thrower
Whether a reader is new to gardening, or wishing to adapt an existing garden for more efficient maintenance, this book offers practical guidance. Illustrated in full colour.
£1.95   0–86242–039–3

Life in the Sun: A guide to long-stay holidays and living abroad in retirement
Nancy Tuft
Every year millions of older people consider either taking long-stay holidays or moving abroad on a more permanent basis. This essential guide examines the pitfalls associated with such a move and tackles topics varying from pets to packing.
£6.95   0–86242–085–7

Out and About: A travel and transport guide

Richard Armitage and John Taylor

A comprehensive source of information on travel and transport for older people and others with limited mobility. Whether planning a trip to the local shops or a journey abroad, this book provides a step-by-step guide to the arrangements that need to be made.

£6.95   0–86242–092-X

HOUSING

An Owner's Guide: Your home in retirement

Foreword by Christopher Chope OBE MP

This definitive guide considers all aspects of home maintenance of concern to retired people and those preparing for retirement, providing advice on heating, insulation and adaptations.

Co-published with the NHTPC.

£2.50   0–86242–095–4

Housing Options for Older People

David Bookbinder

A review of housing options is part of growing older. All the possibilities and their practical implications are carefully considered in this comprehensive guide.

£4.95   0–86242–108-X

To order books, send a cheque or money order to the address below: postage and packing is free. Credit card orders may be made on 081–679 8000.

ACE Books
Age Concern England
PO Box 9
London SW16 4EX

Information factsheets

Age Concern England produces factsheets on a variety of subjects, and among these the following titles may be of interest to readers of this book:

Factsheet 12 *Raising Income or Capital from Your Home*

Factsheet 13 *Older Home Owners: Financial help with repairs*

Factsheet 15 *Income Tax and Older People*

Factsheet 16 *Income Related Benefits: Income and capital*

Factsheet 17 *Housing Benefit and Community Charge Benefit*

Factsheet 19 *Your State Pension and Carrying on Working*

Factsheet 20 *National Insurance Contributions and Qualifying for a Pension*

Factsheet 21 *The Community Charge (Poll Tax) and Older People*

Factsheet 22 *Legal Arrangements for Managing Financial Affairs*

Factsheet 25 *Income Support and the Social Fund*

Factsheet 30 *Leisure Education*

To order factsheets

Single copies are free on receipt of a 9" x 6" sae. If you require a selection of factsheets or multiple copies totalling more than 10, charges will be given on request. A complete set of factsheets is available in a ring binder at the current cost of £30, which includes the first year's subscription. The current cost for an annual subscription for subsequent years is £12. There are different rates of subscription for people living abroad.

Factsheets are revised and updated throughout the year and membership of the subscription service will ensure that your information is always correct.

> For further information, or to order factsheets, write to:
>
> **Information and Policy Department**, Age Concern England, 1268 London Road, London SW16 4ER

We hope you found this book useful. If so, perhaps you would like to receive further information about Age Concern or help us do more for elderly people.

Dear Age Concern
Please send me the details I've ticked below:

other publications ☐   *Age Concern special offers* ☐

volunteer with a local group ☐   *regular giving* ☐

covenant ☐   *legacy* ☐

Meantime, here is a gift of

£ _____ PO/CHEQUE or VISA/ACCESS No _____

NAME (BLOCK CAPITALS) _____

SIGNATURE _____

ADDRESS _____

_____

POSTCODE _____

Please pull out this page and send it to: **Age Concern** (DEPT EM1)
FREEPOST
1268 London Road
no stamp needed **London SW16 4EJ**

Index